FAITH AND CULTURES SERIES

The New Catholicity

Theology between
the Global and the Local

Robert J. Schreiter, C.PP.S.

ORBIS BOOKS

Maryknoll, New York 10545

Seventh Printing, September 2004

Copyright © 1997 by Robert J. Schreiter.
Published by Orbis Books, Maryknoll, New York, U.S.A.

Library of Congress Cataloging in Publication Data

Schreiter, Robert J.
    The new catholicity : theology between the global and the local /
Robert J. Schreiter.
        p.   cm. — (Faith and culture series)
    "This book is a revised edition of lectures given at the
University of Frankfurt in the autumn of 1995"—Introd.
    Includes bibliographical references and index.
    ISBN 1-57075-120-X (alk. paper)
      1. Catholic Church—History—1965-   2. Catholic Church—Doctrines.
3. Christianity and culture. I. Title. II. Series
BX1390.S36   1997
230'.2—dc21
                                                97-1665
                                                 CIP

Contents

Introduction

Local or contextual theologies developed in the 1970s and 1980s in cultures and groups where the prevailing Enlightenment theologies of Europe and North America did not respond to local needs. Thus, outside the Western world and among disenfranchised peoples—women and people of color—in the West, a new kind of theology emerged. It was based on the analysis of social conditions and the issues raised by culture.

By the 1990s important changes had taken place. Politically, the world had moved from a First/Second/Third World division to a multipolar condition where the division was now more than ever between rich and poor. Economically this meant the surge and sweep of a new neoliberal capitalism that pronounced its inevitability even to those who did not want it. Communications technologies compressed time and space in a process known as globalization. Globalization has created a certain homogenization of the world in its wake, but has at the same time unleashed new particularisms: religious protest movements, nativist reassertions of sovereignty, and fundamentalisms of a variety of stripes. These particularisms represent in many instances a new intensification of the local.

What has globalization meant for local theologies, as social relationships are realigned, cultural production is at once homogenized and fractured, and peoples migrate and mix at an unprecedented rate, creating a cultural melange in the urban centers of the world? And in such a dizzying world, is there any place for "universal" theologies, or are these remnants of an obsolete imperial project?

This book looks at the changed world and tracks some of the issues that are reshaping theology today. Theology stands today between the global and the local. The global is not the same as the old universal or perennial theologies. Despite the homogenizing aims of globalization, local situations remain robust in their resistance. And there is no "local" any more that is not touched by powerful outside forces. In fact, the local itself increasingly cannot be defined simply in territorial terms. Theology must find ways of embracing both the global and the local if it is to be a faithful and credible voice for belief.

The first chapter surveys this changed world and its meaning for contextual theologies. After an examination of the forces that together make up globalization, recent work in the sociology of religion and culture theory is used to trace religion's roles in all of this. From this the proposal is made that there are identifiable global theological "flows" (as there are other cultural and information flows) that may be taking the place of the universal theologies of the past. The chapter concludes by examining how religion is presenting itself in the particularisms of today, from fundamentalisms and revanchist policies to reassertion of local value.

To live and act in such a changed world will require new theories of interpretation. The second chapter examines elements of an intercultural hermeneutical theory that might undergird a theology that must live constantly in a multicultural context. Drawing upon intercultural communication theory, salient aspects of such a hermeneutics are then sketched out, as well as the kinds of theological issues such a theory might address and the issues the theory itself raises for theology.

Chapter 3 looks at some of the new theories of culture emerging from postcolonial writing and culture studies, and explores the implications of these theories for theology. With changed theories of culture—where culture can no longer be seen as an integrated trinity of language, custom, and territory—a new theology of culture will also be needed. How does theology give expression to faith in a fragmented, hybridized culture? And what happens to the significance of culture itself for theology?

Put another way, how are religious identities being formed in a globalized world? The concept of syncretism has received much play in recent cultural anthropology, but remains a negatively charged concept in much of theology. Chapter 4 brings to bear recent thought on syncretism in order to explore how religious identities are being shaped in this new world, a world in which people inhabit multiple identities at the same time. Is syncretism simply the other face of inculturation, as Peruvian anthropologist Manuel Marzal has averred?

One part of the world where contextual theologies are becoming of interest—not as objects of exotic study, but as local realities—is contemporary Europe. Chapter 5 explores the social and cultural forces in Europe today that are calling forth contextual theologies. Globalization is having a reflexive effect on Europe itself, as modernity takes on new and unexpected forms. Secularization has not quite turned out to be what Max Weber had expected it to be, and post-Christian society is rife with new religious movements. All of this is happening in a Europe struggling with economic and political reunion after half a century of enmity, a Europe facing immigrations from Asia, Africa, and the

Caribbean that are remaking what have been largely monocultural societies. What will contextual theologies have to take into account in such a changed environment?

Perhaps nowhere have the changes in the world been felt as keenly in contextual theology as in the case of Latin American liberation theologies. The sweep of neoliberal capitalism into Latin America has only exacerbated the very issues of poverty and oppression that liberation theologies have tried to address. The repression of these theologies by the Roman Catholic Church has made the situation even more difficult. In some places (such as South Africa) postures of resistance are giving way to appeals for collaboration in a reconstruction of society. Where might liberation theologies go in this changed situation? Chapter 6 offers an analysis and some proposals regarding what have been among the most creative developments (along with feminist theologies) in theology in the latter half of the twentieth century.

Analysis of communication, culture, identity, and social movements is all well and good—even necessary—for theology, but what will make a theology standing between the global and the local cohere? Chapter 7 proposes that an enlarged concept of catholicity can meet this challenge. The marks of the Church professed in the Nicene Creed—one, holy, catholic, and apostolic—each has responded at different times to crises and challenges in the life of the Church. The oneness of the Church became salient at the time of the Great Schism and in the ecumenical atmosphere after World War II. The holiness of the Church was key at the time of the Donatist controversy as the Church made the transition from a church of martyrs (resistance) to a church of the majority (reconstruction). Apostolicity hung in the balance in the Reformation controversies of the sixteenth century. Today the issue is catholicity. Can the Church of Jesus Christ balance the global and the local, with all the implications implied therein? Catholicity has traditionally been understood as extension throughout the world and the fullness of the faith handed down from the apostles. Now communication—including issues of culture, identity, and social change—becomes the third and necessary addition to the theological concept of catholicity. It is perhaps only by such an addition that some of the struggles so apparent in theology today—about concepts of the Church, appropriate forms of inculturation, commitment to liberation, and possible reconciliation—can be addressed effectively. This theological addendum gives the new catholicity concreteness.

This book is a revised edition of lectures given at the University of Frankfurt in the autumn of 1995. The professors in the department of Catholic theology gathered resources—including some of their own—to fund a chair for "Theologie Interkulturell" in 1985. Unique in the

Federal Republic of Germany, this chair has brought scholars from around the world to share what is happening in their areas in the development of contextual or intercultural theologies. I was honored to be the incumbent for the tenth anniversary of this program. My thanks go to them—Pius Siller, Hans Kessler, Siegfried Wiedenhofer, Johannes Hoffmann, Michael Raschke, Thomas Schreijäck, Josef Hainz, and Franz Josef Stendebach—for their hospitality, their interest, and their engagement. Conversations with others in Frankfurt and beyond helped me clarify my thinking. I am especially grateful to Edmund Arens, Bernhard Dörr, Stefan Heim, Wolfgang Fischer, Michael Kern, Norbert Hintersteiner, and Martin Ried. Thanks, too, to Kenneth O'Malley, who prepared the index. And finally, a word of gratitude to my ever patient editor at Orbis Books, William Burrows.

The Theologie Interkulturell lectures came ten years after the publication of *Constructing Local Theologies*. Those who know that book will recognize the recurrence of many themes, now looked at from a different perspective. This book is a kind of sequel to that earlier work, although it does not parallel it completely. In two places, the discussion of syncretism and the criteria for Christian identity, this book builds directly on that earlier work. The semiotics of culture is developed further here by a proposal to explain how it transmits messages interculturally. In other places, new directions are taken.

As the world has changed, so have contexts. It is hoped that what is offered here will contribute to an ongoing discussion about how to engage in theology creatively and faithfully between the global and the local situations in which it finds itself.

1

Globalization and the Contexts of Theology

THE "CONTEXT" IN CONTEXTUAL THEOLOGY

When contextual theologies first began to appear in the 1970s, their purpose was to articulate a different way of doing theology from that largely practiced in the academy. That latter form of theology strove to present a reflection that was universal in its scope, mirroring the universal message of the Gospel which was the subject of its investigation. Contextual theologies arose because those universal reflections did not reach far enough. They did not take up the issues that were the most pressing in many local circumstances: the burden of poverty and oppression, the struggle to create a new identity after a colonial past, or the question of how to meet the challenge of modernization and the commodification of the economy in traditional culture and village life. The universal theologies were preoccupied with issues not even being raised in local situations, such as the problem of atheism or secularization. In each case the universal theology turned out to be less than universal, unless of course one argues that these local Christian communities were not "mature" or "developed" enough to appreciate genuine theology.

The reaction to such experiences led to a search for what made peoples' experience of the one Christian faith different, so much so that theologies intended to be universal in scope quite plainly failed to be so. The answer seemed to lie in the different contexts in which Christian communities found themselves. Without reducing theological expression to a mere reflection determined by context, theologians in these settings came to realize that, if Christianity was to engage the hearts and minds of believers, then it must take the context that shapes their lives and in which their communities are rooted much more intentionally and seriously. Communities that were struggling principally with questions of identity looked at their contexts as *culture*. This was particularly evident in those parts of the world recently emerged from situations of colonialism, where local identity had been suppressed or denied in favor of an identity imposed by the colonizer. There the question frequently was: does one have to become Western in order to become a Christian? Such reflections were common in Africa, the South Pacific area, places in Asia where Christians were minorities, and among the indigenous peoples of the Americas. On the other hand, communities struggling especially with the need to bring about the transformation of their societies because of poverty, oppression, and racism looked at their contexts as *social structures,* frequently as class structures. It was in such settings that theologies of liberation arose, based on reflections on class (as in Latin America) or race (as in South Africa). There the question frequently was: how is God acting in this time and place, and what are the signs of the coming of God's rule?

What became clear from these contextual theologies was that the universal theologies that had been presented to them were in fact *universalizing* theologies; that is to say, they extended the results of their reflections beyond their own contexts to other settings, usually without an awareness of the rootedness of their theologies within their own contexts. Subsequently, there has been some reflection on how these universalizing theologies are indeed, too, local theologies, and how the Christian Tradition itself might be seen as a series of local theologies. This was not done to depreciate the efforts of theologians straining to touch the heart of the Christian message—certainly a task incumbent on all theologians everywhere. It was, rather, to remind theologians that all human efforts fall far short of the divine mystery.

Throughout this same period, one would hear dismissive remarks about contextual theologies as not being "real" or genuine theology. Such theology was, at best, a hyphenated theology; on this reading, there was theology and then there was Black theology, Asian theology, feminist theology, and liberation theology. Above all these reigned theology as theology, enthroned on its method. But research on Western concepts of rationality and the origins of the Cartesian method provide a more complex and clearly contextual picture. Rationality turns out to be a much denser concept than the high Enlightenment period would have us believe. Its claims to objectivity found their origins in methods that were followed (beginning especially with Descartes) and in the social location of those who were using them. Stephen Toulmin has described that context that gave rise to this idea that truth is best reached by a method that abstracts from its surroundings as much as possible. The experience of the Thirty Years' War, with its battling on doctrinal differences, made such an idea extremely attractive.[1] Research into the origins of modern scientific method as it developed from the seventeenth century gives us a picture of how much who is doing science has contributed to its "objectivity."[2] Courtiers and gentlemen were seen as objective, because the former engaged in science disinterestedly for the sake of the glory of their lords, while the latter were able to do so because they sought no financial gain. With objectivist understandings of rationality no longer wielding the authority they once claimed, rationality itself has come to be seen as something that cannot be established solely by argument, but something that also needs some form of communal validation.[3]

Another way of narrating this same history of the relation of the universal to the local is to describe the move from modernity to postmodernism, from the confidence of reason to the pluralism of rationalities. The need to attend to contexts and cultures, once seen to be the province of those outside the universal, Western tradition, has now become part of the postmodern condition that pervades the West as well. There is, of course, no single definition of postmodernism that has been agreed upon; and some would maintain that postmodernism does not exist apart from modernism itself.[4] But one thing seems clearly to have emerged out of this history: any theology needs to attend both to its contextual and to its universalizing dimensions.

That theology must attend to its context is now much more widely accepted than it would have been in the early 1970s. Be context construed as culture, social structure, or social location, it always plays an important role in framing any theological articulation. Theology must not be reduced to context in a crude contextualism, for then it is likely

---

[1]Stephen Toulmin, *Cosmopolis: The Hidden Agenda of Modernity* (New York: Free Press, 1990).

[2]See among others, Amos Funkenstein, *Theology and the Scientific Imagination* (Princeton: Princeton University Press, 1986); Mario Biagioli, *Galileo Courtier: The Practice of Science in the Culture of Absolutism* (Chicago: University of Chicago Press, 1993); Steven Schapin, *A Social History of Truth: Civility and Science in Seventeenth-Century England* (Chicago: University of Chicago Press, 1994).

[3]This is particularly the case when rationality is seen as a form of rhetoric. See, for example, Calvin Shrag, *The Resources of Rationality: A Response to the Postmodern Challenge* (Bloomington, IN: University of Indiana Press, 1992).

[4]On the problem of postmodernism within theology, see David Tracy, "On Naming the Present," *On Naming the Present: God, Hermeneutics, Church* (Maryknoll, NY: Orbis Books, 1994), 3-24.

to lose its critical edge as it becomes simply a product of its surroundings. The relation to context is always one of intimacy and distance at the same time. It must be rooted in the context, yet be able also to take stock of the context at the same time.

Theology must also have a universalizing function, by which is meant an ability to speak beyond its own context, and an openness to hear voices from beyond its own boundaries. Universalizing is not totalizing, which entails a suppression of difference and a claim to be the sole voice. Theology cannot restrict itself only to its own and immediate context; if the message of what God has done in Christ is indeed Good News for all peoples, then the occurrence of grace in any setting has relevance for the rest of humanity. This understanding of universalization will be developed later in this book in the section on a renewed understanding of the theological concept of catholicity.

The development of the understanding of the "context" in contextual theologies since the 1970s, in which emergent theologies defined themselves over against a universalizing Western theology, has reached an important turning point. World events—some of which have been occurring over a period of time, others of which have happened more abruptly with still not clearly seen consequences—are producing new contexts for theology. As was already noted, context is now a preoccupation for Western theologies in a way that was not the case when non-Western contextual theologies first arose. But changes in the world mean changes in the context anywhere and everywhere, including concomitant changes in theology that is now widely aware of context. Those changes, and thoughts about where they might lead us, are the subject of this book.

That subject will be pursued under the overarching idea of theology being refashioned between the global and local realities in which it finds itself today. This first chapter addresses how contexts are changing and the implications of those changes for a theology between the global and the local. The complex of social processes that is bringing about these changes is known as globalization.

GLOBALIZATION: THE EXTENSION OF MODERNITY AND THE COMPRESSION OF THE WORLD

There is no one accepted definition of globalization, nor is there consensus on its exact description.[5] Nearly all would agree, however,

---

[5]The best single introduction to the globalization discussion is Malcolm Waters, *Globalization* (New York: Routledge, 1995). See also Mike Featherstone (ed.),

that it is about the increasingly interconnected character of the political, economic, and social life of the peoples on this planet. Depending again on how one sees this interconnectedness, it is a phenomenon of the latter part of the twentieth century (the term "globalization" itself first appeared, in English, in 1959), or began with the European voyages of discovery in the late fifteenth century, or dates from the emergence of intercultural trade in the Late Bronze Age.[6] I will be using the term here with the first description in mind—globalization as a phenomenon of the latter part of the twentieth century. Globalization certainly has its antecedents in the European colonizing process, but there are distinct differences in its late twentieth-century manifestation. To understand this, we must first note three processes that have shaped the globalization phenomenon in a special way. The first is political, the second is economic, and the third is technological.

FROM A BIPOLAR TO A MULTIPOLAR WORLD

The first phenomenon, the political, is the collapse of the bipolar political arrangement in 1989. With the planet divided into First and Second Worlds, representing roughly democratic and capitalist versus communist and socialist systems, political life was seen as bipolar and oppositional, symbolized by the threat of mutual nuclear destruction. The poor countries of the southern hemisphere constituted a Third World, sometimes playing the First and Second worlds off against each other, and sometimes being the staging ground for circumscribed, surrogate wars between the two.[7] The surprisingly rapid collapse of this arrangement portended the end of what had been known as the Second

Global Culture: Nationalism, Globalization and Modernity (London: Sage, 1990); Roland Robertson, *Globalization: Social Theory and Global Culture* (London: Sage, 1992); Jonathan Friedman, *Cultural Identity and Global Process* (London: Sage, 1994).

[6]The first position is taken by Peter Beyer, *Religion and Globalization* (London: Sage, 1994); the second, by Immanuel Wallerstein, *The Modern World System: Capitalist Agriculture and the Origins of the European World-Economy in the Sixteenth Century* (New York: Academic Press, 1974); the third, by Friedman, op. cit.

[7]The difficulties of language pose themselves here. The "Third" in Third World has come to mean third-rate or third-class in some circles. When it was adopted as a self-designation by the non-aligned nations at the Bandung Conference in 1955, "Third" meant an alternative to the First or Second Worlds. This also squares with semiotician C. S. Peirce's concept of "thirdness" as taking up a mediating position in the question of signification. Postcolonialist critic Homi Bhabha talks of postcolonial culture being in a "third space," meaning roughly the same thing. For these reasons I am reluctant to abandon the term, realizing at the same time the difficulty of talking about "Third" when the Second appears to have gone out of existence.

World, as some of those countries sought to imitate the First World, whereas others appeared to be sinking into Third World-like poverty. Language of First and Third Worlds is therefore clearly no longer apposite, yet what should replace it is not clear, complicated further as it is by additional factors yet to be mentioned. However our discourse about the world might be reconstructed in the future, the collapse of the distribution of power between two poles has removed as a possibility one prevalent way of thinking, namely, in oppositions. Explaining politics in dyads of opposition, or even dialectically, becomes much more difficult to do. Power has by no means disappeared from the earth; the nations of the erstwhile First World continue to wield it, although paradoxically less so than before. Politically, the world becomes a *multipolar* place that no one yet has been able to map persuasively.[8]

As we shall see, one consequence of the end of this kind of bipolar thinking is a decrease in the importance of territory or contiguity as a way of mapping reality. When one is used to thinking territorially, it becomes difficult to switch to another modality. At the same time, however, space is becoming an increasingly important category in globalization literature, replacing the modern preoccupation with time as a defining category. But space is understood here not as extension but rather as field in which forces come together, clash, and interact. This will be explored later in the discussion of culture.[9]

A SINGLE WORLD ECONOMY

With the collapse of the bipolar reality came the demise, it would seem, of state socialism as an economic possibility. To be sure, the world's most populous nation, China, remains at this writing socialist ideologically, but with what can only be called a mixed economy. The end of socialism in all but a few countries has had two important consequences. First of all, it has allowed for a world-wide expansion of market capitalism, something already well under way before 1989, but certainly intensified since then. This form of capitalism, described by David Harvey as a post-Fordist (i.e., postindustrial) capitalism, and

---

[8]Harvard political scientist Samuel P. Huntington, combining the political, cultural, and religious dimensions, has suggested a map based on what he calls "civilizations." See his "A Clash of Civilizations?" *Foreign Affairs* 72 (Summer, 1993): 22-49. While much discussed, it has not been able to build a strong consensus among students of this problem.

[9]On the new understandings of the relation of time and space, see Scott Lash and John Urry, *Economies of Time and Space* (London: Sage, 1995). On modernity's use of time as a category for dealing with difference, see Johannes Fabian, *Time and the Other* (New York: Columbia University Press, 1983).

called by others neoliberal capitalism, now extends around the world.[10] It is characterized by its ignoring of national boundaries, its ability to move capital quickly, and its engagement in short-term projects that maximize the profit margin. Despite these common characteristics, this form of market capitalism does vary in different parts of the world, as one can see when one compares the capitalist economies and practices of its three major centers, Europe, North America, and Japan. In all its forms, however, it has a tendency to replicate the liberal capitalism of the nineteenth century (hence the epithet neoliberal) and to remove itself as far as possible from all the social constraints developed especially by the social democracies of Europe after the Second World War. Like the new political world, it too is multipolar with the principal centers those already mentioned, but growing ones in South Korea, Southeast Asia, and some of the countries of Latin America.

Attitudes toward this form of capitalism are deeply ambivalent. On the one hand it has generated great amounts of new wealth which, were they distributed more evenly, would do much to ease the poverty of the majority of the world's population. Indeed, some countries in Latin America and Asia are beginning to have the resources to meet the needs of more of their citizens than in any time in the past. But the negative aspects of this form of capitalism loom more starkly than the positive. Some people are enriched fabulously, but many more are not only not better off, but are actually being driven deeper into poverty and misery. This is caused partially by global capitalism's quest for short-term profit, a quest that precludes long-term commitment to a people and a place; and partially by the destruction of traditional and small-scale societies and economies by the centrality of the market. The 1996 United Nations Development Program notes that with the increase in wealth, the disparity between rich and poor is growing worse in nearly all parts of the world, with roughly 20 percent enjoying the fruits of global capitalism, and the rest struggling to hold their ground and slipping away into deeper poverty. If there is a new bipolarization of the world today, it is not between capitalist and socialist, or even between North and South. It is between those who profit from global capitalism and those who are excluded and, increasingly, ignored by the rich.

The second consequence of the end of socialism is that it becomes more difficult, if not downright impossible, to imagine alternative social and economic forms that can coexist with global capitalism. On the one hand, market-driven economies, with their all-devouring tendency, wish to promote this sense of inevitability, to free any remaining con-

---

[10]David Harvey, *The Condition of Postmodernity* (Oxford: Basil Blackwell, 1989).

straints on the market. On the other, alternative schemes have to be realistic enough to be able to engage the current situation. Simply to call for an end to global capitalism is something likely to fall on deaf ears. Repeating the nostrums of the past, but only shouting them more loudly, will likewise not move things forward. For all of communist socialism's defects, it did hold out the possibility that the humane values of socialism (an economy based on sharing rather than accumulation and greed, a guarantee of meeting basic needs of all citizens) could be realized, and that there might be a way for traditional societies to experience progress in their material state without a corrosion of their values, as has occurred historically under capitalism. This led to intense discussions in Latin America and elsewhere among those committed to the economic and social liberation of their peoples. It is a subject to which we will return in chapter 6.

NEW COMMUNICATIONS TECHNOLOGIES

The third phenomenon, the technological, is the advancement in communications. Thanks to the new communications technologies, messages and information can now be sent around the world with near instantaneity. Air travel makes the movement of persons and cargo rapid and relatively inexpensive. Just as the first two phenomena of a multipolar world and an interconnected single economic system have changed how we think of our world, so too the communications revolution of the second half of the twentieth century has reshaped how we perceive time and space. The communications technologies make possible a networking that increasingly eludes hierarchical control; network has replaced hierarchy as a social model for communication. Travel possibilities allow for the movement of peoples in such a way as to reconfigure societies, allowing for migrations on a massive scale. These are creating societies where cultures come into contact with each other and result both in conflict and in new possibilities.

The convergence of these three phenomena—a multipolar world, global capitalism, and communications technologies—create what is known as globalization. In defining globalization, I would like to draw upon the reflections of two sociologists who have reflected not only on globalization, but on the role of religion within globalization as well: Roland Robertson and Peter Beyer. Globalization, as defined here, is the extension of the effects of modernity to the entire world, and the compression of time and space, all occurring at the same time.[11]

---

[11]The first part of this definition, on extension, is from Beyer, op. cit., and the second part, on compression, is from Robertson, op. cit.

GLOBALIZATION AS EXTENSION

Globalization is therefore first of all about extension. It extends the effects of modernity throughout the entire world via the communications technologies that create a network for information flow. Computers, modems, faxes, and the Internet make possible this swift transfer. Modernity as a process is tied up with the achievement of Enlightenment ideals and the growth of capitalism. It has been marked by greater individual autonomy and an improvement in the material state of being. Positively, modernization means increased material prosperity, better health care, expanded opportunities for formal education, an increase in personal freedom and individuality, and a liberation from many traditional constraints. But it has its negative side as well, to be seen in materialism, personhood defined by one's capacity to produce and consume material goods, the erosion or relativization of values, and an anomic individualism. Because modernity promises greater autonomy but exacts great costs in terms of traditional values and relationships, people feel an ambivalence when they are caught up in the whirlwind (or maelstrom, if you will) of globalization. It is in the context of this ambivalence that we must theologize, in a force field in which people are at once attracted and repelled by modernity.

The spread of modernization through the extension of its first product, Western culture, creates powerful homogenizing systems that often function in much the same way from country to country. The global system of capital formation, development, and transfer is one such system, symbolized in the interconnected stock exchange that now runs twenty-four hours a day. International science and medicine function in a similar fashion, one in which the same standards are maintained across countries and cultures. Postsecondary education is increasingly being brought into the same systemic patterns. While there are still local and national variations, homogenized patterns are becoming stronger and stronger as time goes on.

These global systems are driven by values of innovation, efficiency, and technical rationality. Again, these are deeply ambivalent values. Innovation connotes improvement, something nearly everyone would welcome. But innovation without a clear goal becomes change for its own sake, or change to create new markets or to stimulate desire. Efficiency can mean less drudgery; but efficiency without effectiveness can become narrow and abstract, even deadly. Technical rationality has the advantage of providing clear purpose and procedure, but it can become profoundly dehumanizing.

The values that drive global systems are matched by ideals that are held up to those who encounter these global systems. Beyer identifies these ideals as progress, equality, and inclusion.[12] As with values, these ideals have two faces. Progress (as with value, innovation) connotes improvement, but change in itself does not mean betterment. Equality is an important Enlightenment ideal for all of those who have suffered from a hierarchical society. But equality must be more than an abstract ideal. What does it mean concretely? Equality of opportunity? A common ceiling for achievement? A ruthless leveling of any difference? Inclusion touches upon the deepest human yearnings for belonging. But if inclusion means a complete erasure of difference, does it still remain an ideal?

What all of this points to is that neither values nor ideals lead to a better society in and of themselves. Larger questions about the goal or *telos* of society must be answered. As Robertson has pointed out, globalization in itself does not provide the answers.

The experience of homogenization in global cultures is heightened by a hyperculture (that is, an overarching cultural proposal that is in itself not a complete culture) based on consumption and marked by icons of consumption derived from the most powerful of the homogenizing cultures, that of the United States. These icons include clothing (T-shirts, denim jeans, athletic shoes), food (McDonald's, Coca-Cola), and entertainment (American TV, films, videos, and music).[13]

Homogenizing as these systems might be, they do not end up homogenizing local cultures altogether. It is increasingly evident that local cultures receive the elements of the hyperculture and reinterpret them in some measure. Producers of goods know this and often adjust their products accordingly. McDonald's menus and even the formula for Coca-Cola are varied to suit local tastes; pop music takes on local accents. In other instances, the products of the hyperculture foster a certain cosmopolitanism, a sense of participating in something larger, grander, and more powerful than our immediate situation. The current craze for paraphernalia from the Chicago Bulls basketball team does not necessarily bespeak a keen interest in American professional basketball. It may, rather, reflect a desire to participate in the mystique of something distant and powerful. Eating at McDonald's may be a relatively expensive option open only to the wealthy in poor countries, whereas McDonald's may be considered a quick and inexpensive alternative for those living in wealthy countries. The hyperculture of consumption is not a culture in itself; it represents elements that at-

---

[12]The concepts of values and ideals in global systems are both taken from Beyer, op. cit.

[13]George Ritzer, *The McDonaldization of Society* (Thousand Oaks, CA: Pine Forge, 1993). Others speak of a "Coca-Colonization" of the world.

tach themselves to and lodge themselves in local cultures in a variety of ways.

The extension of modernity in globalization is not simply the imperial reach of the West in a new guise. What becomes ever clearer is that the globalization process creates plural modernities. This is particularly evident in Asia. In Japan, for instance, modernization has brought not secularization so much as new religions, the latest wave of which address personal therapeutic needs. Modernity introduced into China seems to help spur a revival of Christianity and to some extent Islam, although other internal factors of China's immediate past history must also be taken into account. Such creation of modernities would be consistent with other forms of production in the globalization process: plural forms that resemble one another yet are embedded in and reflect local cultures.

GLOBALIZATION AS COMPRESSION

Globalization not only extends the effects of modernity, and with it elements of Western culture. It has a compressing effect as well. Technological innovations compress both our sense of time and our sense of space. Events happening around the world are now experienced instantaneously. We are participating in world history in a new way as we experience it simultaneously through CNN and Star Television. We are able to maintain contacts and relationships through the telephone and e-mail that could have been sustained previously only by occasional postal correspondence. The rapidity of movement (and a capitalism always in search of "progress" and innovation) disparages attaching any significance to the past and makes the future ever more short-term. Time becomes a present with an edge of future, reminding us of the constant obsolescence of the past.

Our sense of space is also compressed, symbolized in the computer chip. Boundaries between states become increasingly insignificant in the flow of information and capital. The formation of new confederations such as the European Union and the establishment of trading blocks undercut claims of sovereignty of the state. The movement of peoples, especially rural peoples in search of the benefits of modernization, makes the meaning of home as ancestral place less significant. A third of all the people living in the city of Frankfurt in Germany, for example, do not hold German passports. If boundaries play an important role in the semiotics of identity by helping us define who we are by who we are not, they are now so crisscrossed by globalization processes that they seem to have lost their identity-conferring power.

THE GLOBAL AND THE LOCAL

Throughout the discussion of globalization as extension and as compression, emphasis has been placed on how the powerful homogenizing forces reshape the local situation. It must be noted at the same time that the local situation is not some inert, passive object upon which globalization plays itself out. We saw that the interaction between the global and the local has not meant a simple replication of Western modernity; it has, indeed, generated plural modernities that may resemble the Western variety, but nonetheless remain distinct. Much of the tension, conflict, and struggle that globalization generates grows out of the resistance that the local is able to muster. Globalization, as we have seen, is both enticing in its promises and abhorrent in some of its consequences. The local situation seldom can keep globalizing forces out altogether (and frequently does not want to), and so it is inevitably changed by the encounter. The local situation may indeed feel itself overwhelmed by the global, and sometimes that feeling is also fact. Intercultural encounter on whatever scale is frequently conflictual; calls for dialogue and mutuality often express more hope than reality. But local situations are not powerless either. They work out all kinds of arrangements, from syncretic borrowing to living in subaltern or dual systems.[14] These will be taken up in more detail below in chapter 4. But what happens is that the important moment for cultural (and theological) production becomes the line of encounter between the global and the local, where the two come up against each other. Roland Robertson describes this encounter of the global and the local as "glocalization."[15] As we shall see below, some of the most salient features in religion and theology today can best be described from the vantage point of the glocal. Neither the global, homogenizing forces nor the local forms of accommodation and resistance can of themselves provide an adequate explanation of these phenomena. It is precisely in their interaction that one comes to understand what is happening.

REFLEXIVITY AND RISK

One may hold that many of the processes described here are simply those of a vastly speeded up modernization. But globalization can-

---

[14]See the discussion of the range of possibilities in Robert Schreiter, *Constructing Local Theologies* (Maryknoll, NY: Orbis Books, 1985), chapter 7.

[15]Roland Robertson, "Glocalization: Time-Space and Homogeneity-Heterogeneity," in Scott Lash and Roland Robertson (eds.), *Global Modernities* (London: Sage, 1995).

not be reduced to modernization. Most would agree that modernization worked through a process of center-periphery, where the West
drew raw material resources from the periphery to its center and in
turn, through colonialism, reproduced its own social patterns in the
name of civilization or development. Globalization, however, is not a
process that affects just the former periphery or other, still untouched
areas. It affects also the West itself in a process of reflexivity[16]
whereby the outflowing of modernization curves back upon the West.
This is most evidenced in the influx of former colonial people into
Britain, France, and Portugal, creating multicultural societies in previously monocultural situations. But what reflexivity brings as well is a
sense of contingency or risk that has long been the experience of
countries on the periphery. The risks caused by pharmaceuticals and
chemical accidents, but especially by the acts of terrorism of those
profoundly opposed to the inroads that modernity has made into traditional societies (be they militia forces in the United States who see the
United Nations at the center of a great conspiracy, or extremists in
North Africa battling France, or Middle Eastern fundamentalists battling the West in general) create a profound sense of unease and contingency in lives that modernity had promised to insulate from such
vulnerabilities.

This reflexivity is one way to explain the emergence of postmodernism in the West, the fact that the West is now experiencing the
same kinds of ambivalences (or contradictions) felt by the rest of the
world. There may be no direct equivalencies in the ambivalences, but
the *experience* of risk that arises out of ambivalence can be considered
as being more or less the same. When drugs injected to stop one dis-
ease start another, when no number of security measures can thwart
the terrorist—these experiences undermine any "master narrative" of
what society can be counted on to be. When globalization offers only
progress that provides no *telos* that can explain why things have come
to be as they are; when the efficiency promised cannot be delivered;
when the technical rationality does not address the sense of dread and
fear that continues to arise, postmodernism in one or other of its forms
will likely emerge. It may express itself in an anarchism that denies all
value, or in a burrowing into a specific community or way of life as an
enclave providing insulation against the contingencies one faces. Or,

---

[16]See the discussion in Ulrich Beck, Anthony Giddens, and Scott Lash, *Reflexive Modernization* (Stanford, CA: Stanford University Press, 1994). This builds on
the work of Giddens on the concept of reflexivity and the work of Ulrich Beck on
the return of risk to Western society. See on the latter Ulrich Beck, *The Risk Society: Toward a New Modernity* (London: Sage, 1992).

in the flood of information, it may seek the authoritarian ways of a guru who appears to be able to make the whole thing stop.

For that reason, the investigation of where theology might go is best done not within the framework of postmodernism (this would provide mainly an interaction with symptoms, as deconstructionist and communitarian postmodern theologies tend to do),[17] but within the larger frame of globalization. One must be able not just to account for postmodern theologies as forms of contextual theology found in the West, but also to situate them within the larger situation of what is happening to context in the world today.

It is to that account of religion and theology within a globalized world that we now turn.

RELIGION AND THEOLOGY IN A GLOBALIZED WORLD

If there are global systems in economics, science, medicine, and education, is religion a global system as well? Religion is certainly pervasive through most of the world, and its prominence may even be on the increase under the pressures of globalization, if one takes into account the rise of New Age and other free-form types of spirituality in North America and Europe; Pentecostalism among Christians in Africa and Latin America; fundamentalism in Judaism, Christianity, Islam, and Hinduism in a broad swath across northern Africa, the Middle East, and the Indian subcontinent; new religious sects in Buddhism in Thailand and Japan; and ties with nationalism in Hinduism and Islam in Central Asia, the Indian subcontinent, and Indonesia. Religion as such appears to be on the rise, but does not qualify as a global system as do the other systems already mentioned. There are several reasons for this. First of all, these religious resurgences lack the general uniformity that mark systems in economics, science, and medicine. Second, they are not driven by these systems' values and ideals. Innovation and progress may be replaced with other values and ideals such as faithful adherence to law and tradition. Hierarchy, in the sense of fitting into a divine order of things, may be more important than Western notions of equality, and boundaries of purity may take precedence over ideals of inclusion. Third, they do not have levels of organization based on the new communications technologies as do the other systems. There is no central organization for Buddhism, Judaism, or Islam. The World Council of Churches represents many Christian bodies, but not all of

---

[17]For an overview of postmodern theologies, see Terrence Tilley et al., *Postmodern Theologies* (Maryknoll, NY: Orbis Books, 1995).

them, and would not consider itself a global system. The Roman Catholic Church in the policies of John Paul II may aspire to be a global system, but it cannot enforce the control on all levels and to all extents that would mark such a system. Beyer maintains that the forces of modernization privatize religion and therefore cannot make religion a player in global systems. This assumes that modernities in all parts of the world follow the secularization pattern mapped out by Max Weber, as they apparently do not in Japan and South Asia. It is uncertain whether secularization follows the trajectory that Weber envisioned even in Europe, a question that will be taken up again in chapter 5.

One may agree with Beyer that religion does not function as a global system, even while not accepting that privatization is the cause of this. It may be that even those religious traditions aspiring to universality do not envision universality as operating in the manner of the global systems. At the same time, religion can be a powerful and unified force in smaller scale levels such as a nation or a region. Indeed, one of Huntington's civilizations, Islamic civilization, was held together by religious belief and practice.

Where might theology fit into all of this, as it interacts with its contexts? Theology in a world shaped by globalization finds itself between the global and the local. In what follows, how theology interacts with both the global and the local will be explored. The global interaction will be considered in terms of global theological flows; the local interaction in terms of cultural logics.

GLOBAL THEOLOGICAL FLOWS

"Flow" is a term that has come to be used in sociology, anthropology, and communications science to denote cultural and ritual movements, a circulation of information that is patently visible yet hard to define.[18] Flows move across geographic and other cultural boundaries, and, like a river, define a route, change the landscape, and leave behind sediment and silt that enrich the local ecology. Paul Gilroy employs the idea of a cultural flow to describe the circulation of African culture around the Atlantic basin.[19] While African culture can be said to have begun on the African continent, forced and voluntary migration has spread that culture to Latin America, the Caribbean region, North America, and Great Britain. The flow has not been one-way, however. African

---

[18]See, for example, Manuel Castell, *The Informational City* (Oxford: Basil Blackwell, 1989).

[19]Paul Gilroy, *The Black Atlantic: Modernity and Double Consciousness* (Cambridge, MA: Harvard University Press, 1994).

Americans were instrumental in awakening black consciousness and black nationalism in Africa. Jamaican music flowed into North America where it was reborn as rap music. The first pan-African congresses were held in Europe. Thus, one must speak of a cultural flow as a circulation around the Atlantic when one wishes to speak of African culture. The Atlantic then becomes the "Black Atlantic." Gilroy himself is emblematic of this: born in Great Britain of Jamaican parentage, he now divides his time between Britain and the United States.

The global theological flow, then, is a kind of circulating movement. It is perhaps best understood in terms of Peter Beyer's concept of antisystemic global movements.[20] We have seen that religion cannot be seen as a global system in the strict sense of the term. However, Beyer proposes, it can mobilize antisystemic feeling in cultures, especially when global systems fail to live up to their ideals of progress, equality, and inclusion. Religion's holism and commitment to particular cultures give it moral power against what appear to be alienating and impersonal global systems. In its antisystemic action, religion engages in what Beyer calls "religious performance," i.e., providing religious answers to problems created by global systems. In so doing, religion as an antisystemic movement can provide the *telos* that a global system lacks, offering a vision of coherence and order. But giving a religious answer to an economic or political problem may result in a lack of specificity either to the problem or to the setting in which it is manifest.

Global theological flows, then, are theological discourses that, while not uniform or systemic, represent a series of linked, mutually intelligible discourses that address the contradictions or failures of global systems. They are theological discourses, that is, they speak out of the realm of religious beliefs and practices. They are not uniform or systemic, because of their commitment to specific cultural and social settings. Yet they are intelligible to discourses in other cultural and social settings that are experiencing the same failure of global systems and who are raising the same kind of protest.

I would suggest that there are at least four such global theological flows discernible in the world today as linked, mutually intelligible discourses: theologies of (1) liberation, (2) feminism, (3) ecology, and (4) human rights.

Theologies of Liberation

Within a very brief time of less than twenty years (made no doubt briefer by communications technologies), theologies of liberation were

---

[20]Beyer, op. cit., 96-110.

able to become a truly global theological flow. Originating in Latin America, but since spread to oppressed people everywhere, these theologies represent what Gustavo Gutiérrez has called "the irruption of the poor." They point to the consummate failure of the global economic system to bring relief to the poor, and to the fact that in so many places the poor are being driven by that same system into even deeper misery. Liberation theologians hold up a holistic vision of the Reign of God as an antidote to the fragmenting and alienating acids of capitalism. As theologies of liberation have developed and spread to Africa and to Asia, they have deeply differentiated the faces of poverty for the rest of the world and have had a profound influence on the other global theological flows to be discussed here. Their support for such social virtues as solidarity and commitment to the local situation (*inserción*) and their struggle to making the poor subjects of their own history have brought them into conflict with political and ecclesiastical forces. It is their unstinting denunciation of the plight of the poor and the failure of the rich that have made them such a force to contend with.

Changed political and economic circumstances as well as repressive political and ecclesiastical policies toward theologies of liberation have brought them to a new threshold of challenge. This has come about just as they have been consolidating their strength, as is evident in the fifty-volume library on liberation theology and the publication of *Mysterium Liberationis*.[21] With the CEHILA project, they are revising how church history is being written and transmitted. The challenges facing liberation theology, especially in its Latin American varieties, will be taken up in chapter 6.

What should be noted here is how theologies of liberation have operated as a global theological flow. They began in Latin America, but were quickly imitated elsewhere. Linkages were established early on between the various regional discourses in organizations such as the Ecumenical Association of Third World Theologians (EATWOT). Using Beyer's construct, the theologies of liberation had a strong antisystemic tone, which brought them quickly into conflict with the powers they addressed, both political and ecclesiastical. Their solutions to poverty and oppression are examples of religious performance—largely religious answers to economic and social problems. To be sure, their analyses explored the roots of the problems and found more than economic causes. But poverty needs alleviation on the material, economic level. And social oppression needs concrete proposals for the restructuring of society.

---

[21]Selected volumes of this library have been published in English in the Theology and Liberation series of Orbis Books. An abridged version of *Mysterium Liberationis* appeared in English, also from Orbis Books, in 1993.

Liberation theologies have been at their strongest, *pace* Beyer, when they have been related to concrete communities and problems. The fact that they can give hope, mobilize the poor, and prompt even some of the rich to enter into solidarity with them is testimony to their power and, as theologies, of their efficaciousness.[22]

Feminist Theologies

Feminist theologies constitute a second global theological flow. Beginning in the United States out of and alongside of the women's emancipation movement of the 1960s, they have spread to all continents. While they are accused by some of being an unwanted U.S. export (via the channels of globalization!), subsequent literature and world conferences (such as the one held in Beijing in 1994) have shown that feminism has been taken to heart by women and supportive men everywhere. American feminism has revolved around two foci: equal access to society and an equal stature with men, and an exploration of the distinctive gifts of women. As feminism has spread, it has taken on different issues and concerns, from female genital mutilation in Africa to status questions in India. There are many common concerns, such as patriarchy, yet the same issue may be approached from different perspectives, such as whether or not women should be veiled in Islam.[23]

As a global theological flow, feminist theologies point to the failure of global systems to live up to the values of equality and inclusion. How those systems fail is wide-ranging, from failure to provide basic necessities to blocking educational, political, and social advancement. Feminist theologies work on several levels to address these failures: by analyzing the situations and systems of oppression, by reconstructing theological histories to foreground women and lift the silence, by constructing theologies as resources for women's identity. Inasmuch as a disproportionate number of the world's poor are women, there are close links also to theologies of liberation.

As a global theological flow, feminist theologies are interesting for a number of reasons. Whereas theologies of liberation began in Latin America and have come to attract both support and criticism in the richer Northern hemisphere, feminist theologies have made the journey in the other direction. Second, the experience of Third World women

---

[22]Beyer, op. cit., 135-59.

[23]See Helen Watson, "Women and the Veil: Personal Responses to Global Process," Akbar Ahmed and Hastings Donnan (eds.), *Islam, Globalization and Postmodernity* (New York: Routledge, 1994), 141-59.

and women of minority population groups in North America have con-scientized and reshaped North Atlantic feminist theologies. Here the globalization phenomenon, provoking a reflexivity in centers of West-ern culture and modernity, is clearly in evidence. And finally, because of the ubiquity of feminist theologies (since women are oppressed in both rich and poor countries), the global flow of feminist theologies can claim to be something of a universal discourse.

Theologies of Ecology

Peter Beyer gives an extensive treatment of theologies of ecology as they emerged and developed in the World Council of Churches' pro-gram of Justice, Peace and the Integrity of Creation.[24] Environmental degradation was a cause taken up early by religious groups. Beyer pre-sents the theological ecology movement as a prime example of reli-gious performance, providing a moral and religious answer to a biolog-ical and chemical problem. While antisystemic movements work only through persuasion and not through coercion, the ecological movement was successful in bringing about protective and regulatory legislation in a number of countries. The Rio Summit in 1992 did not produce the results for which its planners had hoped, something which also shows the limits of antisystemic persuasion. As Beyer points out, the ecologi-cal cause is ideally suited for what is being called here a global theo-logical flow: it is holistic, it addresses issues that affect everyone, and failure to address these issues means catastrophe for all.

Theologies of Human Rights

The fourth global theological flow is that of theologies of human rights. As was the case for feminist theologies, detractors of theologies of human rights originally charged that human rights were a First World export, imposed upon cultures where they had not been known and were not appropriate. Human rights groups that would then form in those countries were seen as being under the influence of outside, sub-versive forces. The question of the cultural origins of the human rights discourses continues to be raised, and such groups continue to experi-ence oppression, but the language of human rights appears to be pre-vailing.[25] And, as with feminist theologies, theologies of human rights

---

[24]Beyer, op. cit., 206-24.

[25]For a review of how human rights issues and human rights theology are faring in the world, see the three-volume symposium edited by Johannes Hoffmann, *Begründung von Menschenrechten aus der Sicht unterschiedlicher Kulturen; Univer-*

address especially the failure of global systems to reach the ideals of equality and inclusion.

An important development in this global theological flow is the effort to articulate and adopt an interreligious global ethic that can serve as a common charter for integrated action among religions on behalf of world peace and the promotion of humanity. Hans Küng was an early leader in this movement on the Christian side,[26] and the cause has been taken up by such interfaith organizations as the Council for a Parliament of the World's Religions and the World Conference on Religion and Peace.[27]

This global theological flow is at an earlier stage of development than the first three mentioned, all of which go back to the early 1970s. It differs from the other global theological flows in that, in order to promote its agenda, it hopes to engage religion systemically at the level of leadership.

Global Theological Flows as "Universal" Theology

The discourses of liberation, feminism, ecology, and human rights as global theological flows address the contradictions and failures of global systems. Critics of these discourses point out that they are often better at denouncing what they do not like than at providing positive solutions, and that when solutions are proffered (especially in discourses of liberation and ecology) they do not engage the concrete problems effectively. At the same time, one can see that their rhetoric and the strategies that they do choose are conditioned by the fact that they perceive the systemic nature of the problems they address and they select appropriate antisystemic practices. These are issues that will be returned to in chapter 6.

Because these global theological flows are so ubiquitous, they can lay claim to being the new "universal" theologies. They are not universal for the reasons claimed by Enlightenment theologies. They are universal in their ubiquity and in their addressing of universal, systemic problems affecting nearly everyone in the world. Each is rooted in its own context, but these four flows enjoy a mutual intelligibility within their discourses and to a great extent even among them. As we look for

sale Menschenrechten im Widerspruch der Kulturen; Die Vernunft in der Kulturen —Das Menschenrecht auf kultureigene Entwicklung (Frankfurt: IKO Verlag, 1991–95).

[26]Hans Küng, *Global Responsibility: In Search of a New World Ethic* (New York: Crossroad, 1991).

[27]Hans Küng and Karl-Josef Kuschel, *A Global Ethic: The Declaration of the Parliament of the World's Religions* (New York: Continuum, 1994).

new models of universality that are not simply the extension of one culture or one rationality (however excellent or commendable these may be), it is worth attending to these global theological flows as possible ways of articulating the universal. This is something to which we will return in the discussion of catholicity in chapter 7.

CULTURAL LOGICS

In the discussion of globalization above, it was noted that a paradoxical effect takes place as the global meets the local. Even as globalizing processes homogenize the world, they create at the same time a heightened sense of the particular. This attention to the particular and to the local takes on a considerable variety of forms which can range from accommodation of the global to an assertive resistance to it. It was noted above that Roland Robertson has described these phenomena as glocalization. Jonathan Friedman has given perhaps the most attention to the phenomena in delineating what he calls cultural logics, ways that cultures choose to respond to the pressures of globalization.[28] What I wish to do here is to adapt his thinking by looking at three kinds of cultural logic that are animating theological strategies today. These are: antiglobalism, ethnification, and primitivism. Each of these chooses certain strategies to reassert the local in the face of the global.

Antiglobalism

Antiglobalism is an attempt to retreat from the onslaught of globalizing forces altogether. The retreat is not a complete withdrawal, however; it is a retreat on modern terms (as an exercise of choice) and usually relies on modern means to achieve it (such as communications technologies or modern weaponry in acts of terrorism). The retreat is a strategic one in that it often includes a counterattack against the forces of globalization. In antiglobal strategies certain values and icons become signifiers of a boundary drawn and identity formed against the corrosive values and seductive icons of global systems. The antiglobal values and icons are often enshrined in rituals that provide means for building group solidarity among adherents to an antiglobal point of view. Antiglobalism is manifest in theology in two forms: fundamentalism and revanchism.

The term "fundamentalism" is frequently used to cover a wide range of differing conservative responses to modernity and to global-

---

[28]Friedman, op. cit.

ization. Such a generalization masks the range of those responses and hinders our understanding of them. Fundamentalism is understood here as an act of resistance to globalization, marked by signifiers that contradict the direction being taken by globalization (and modernization). The strategy calls also for the establishment of an alternative order. In the choice of signifiers that mark the stance against globalization, fundamentalism is a version of "credo quia absurdum." This is evident in the original use of the term fundamentalism to refer to the five "fundamentals" of American conservative Protestant faith. The five fundamentals—the inerrancy of the Scriptures, the virginal conception of Jesus, substitutionary atonement, the bodily resurrection of Jesus, and his bodily return in the Second Coming—were chosen not because they summed up the essence of Christian faith but because they most contradicted modernist sensibility. The reconstruction of "true faith" in fundamentalism chooses selected items to serve as boundary markers of who is in and who is out. For Archbishop Lefebvre and his followers, the Vatican II Decree on Religious Freedom represented the abomination, and so elements from Pius IX's *Syllabus of Errors* were reasserted. Pius X, the opponent of modernism, became a totemic figure for the rejection of the post-Vatican II reality, with adherence to the Missal of Paul V providing the ritual for group solidarity.[29]

Fundamentalism comes in many forms. Perhaps most talked about today is Islamic fundamentalism, although fundamentalisms appear also in Christianity, Judaism, and Hinduism. Islamic fundamentalism is a strong vehicle for resentment against modernity and against globalization and the West from which it springs. It offers a holism (at least in group solidarity, and putatively in belief) that the fragmented modern and postmodern world do not provide. Because fundamentalisms are so pervasive, they may appear to be similar to global theological flows. But they lack fundamental characteristics of those flows: they are by nature sectarian and are not mutually intelligible discourses. They show the passion of antisystemic protest, but do not work in any coalitions.

A second form of antiglobalism is revanchism, an attempt to regain territory that has been lost. In this logic, priority is given to centraliza-

---

[29]On fundamentalism, see the multivolume work that has been published out of the American Academy of Arts and Sciences Project on Fundamentalisms edited by Martin E. Marty and R. Scott Appleby (Chicago: University of Chicago Press, 1991–95), notably the first and the final volumes, *Fundamentalisms Observed* and *Fundamentalisms Comprehended*. Note the plural use of the term, a recognition that there is no single or univocal way of understanding it. For a history of the beginnings of Christian fundamentalism, see Dominic V. Monty, "World Out of Time: Origins of the Fundamentalist Movement," *New Theology Review* 1 (May, 1988): 5-20.

tion and control directed against globalizing patterns of a multipolar (and therefore, decentralized) world marked by networking rather than a hierarchical command structure. In this logic it is a matter of regaining ground thought to have been lost. There is not the wholesale rejection of modernity found in fundamentalism; indeed, much of the modern world is embraced. Values and icons are used in revanchism as well, but more as symptomatic of how the world needs to be reclaimed so that it will not be lost again. The antiglobalism of revanchism is not fundamentalistic and not necessarily reactionary. In many ways it sets out to provide a *telos* for the world. Its greatest problem is with the centrifugal nature of change and the inability to control and direct movement. It recognizes the devaluation of most values and wishes to reassert a certain vision of and for the world.

An example of revanchism is what would appear to be part of the policy of the latter part of the pontificate of John Paul II. Episcopal appointments of those who are unswervingly loyal to the Vatican take priority over local wishes. The power of episcopal conferences and anything that would diminish the centralized power of the Vatican is called into question. The icons are about the control of social and cultural reproduction: issues of human sexuality (the reproduction of the species) and who may be admitted to the clergy (the social reproduction of the Church). Attitudes toward the globalization of the world are ambivalent. In terms of the global theological flows, there has been a hostility to liberation theologies and a resistance to feminism, but a passionate commitment to human rights. There seems to be little trust in what is emerging as globalized means of communication. Hierarchical means are reasserted.

As we have seen, there is much to be criticized in what is happening in globalization, and its totalizing qualities make selective resistance difficult. Revanchism is one strategy for selective engagement that tries to capture control of the leadership of globalizing trends and direct them in a certain way. The difficulty is that the very nature of globalization makes identifying leadership extremely difficult. In a world that is by definition multipolar, and whose mode of communication is through networking rather than through hierarchy, capturing control becomes, perhaps, an elusive ideal.

Ethnification

Ethnification is the process of rediscovering a forgotten identity based on one's cultural ties. It is about the assertion of local identity, especially amid the experience of social change and cultural instability. In places like Africa at the end of the colonial period after the Second

World War, new national identities had to be articulated. The identity of the colonial masters had to be shaken off. Previously, in countries where independence had been preceded by struggle against the colonizers, being against the colonizer had provided sufficient identity in ethnically plural territories. Now, with the masters gone, the new nations had to find new sources of identity. A similar process began occurring in the former Soviet Union after its dissolution in 1991. With the unprecedented migration of peoples today, groups who had never thought much before about identity are now sometimes going through a process of hyperethnification, whereby they identify with their ethnicity more passionately than they had when living at home. Ethnogenesis, one of the forms of ethnification, is the birth of a new ethnic identity. New ethnic identities are formed as coalitions of migrants create Latino, pan-Asian or pan-African identities in the cities of Europe and North America.[30]

Ethnification involves memory, and memory is necessarily selective and creative, since any group involved in ethnification by definition lives in changed social circumstances. As we shall see in chapter 3, identity becomes an issue only when other things become problematic. In the case of ethnicity called forth by the homogenizing powers of globalization, what is selected to assert ethnicity is often oppositional to the globalizing forces as a way of asserting difference. The selection process can be highly creative. For example, native peoples in western Canada are going through a process of reconstructing an identity shattered by the encounter with European settlers. Much of their language and many of their customs have been lost, and so they borrow freely from neighboring and even distant peoples in order to supplement their own tradition. In cases of ethnogenesis, elements become emphasized that may not even have been part of the original identity, or ideas are appropriated that become the basis for a new identity. José Vasconcelos' concept of the "raza cósmica," to describe the new people emerging in Mexico from the mixing of native and Spanish heritages, is an example of such ethnogenesis.[31]

Establishing ethnic identity, then, is rarely an easy task. Mixing or hybridization is normally the actual case; purity in identity is hard to come by. Moreover, the instability in the situation that raised the iden-

---

[30]Some of the implications for ethnicity are explored in more detail in Robert J. Schreiter, "Ethnicity and Nationality as Contexts for Religious Experience," in Peter Phan (ed.), *Ethnicity, Nationality and Religious Experience* (Lanham, MD: University Press of America, 1995), 9-28.

[31]Roberto S. Goizueta, "La Raza Cósmica: The Vision of José Vasconcelos," *Journal of Hispanic/Latino Theology* 1 (February, 1994): 9-28. It is interesting to note how the meaning of the term itself has changed in the course of time.

tity question in the first place is likely to lead to a hyperdifferentiation of identities. Frequently, in places such as Australia or North America, the arrival of new immigrants asserting their ethnic identity will cause residents of much longer term to reassert ethnic identities largely forgotten or fallen into disuse.

It is easy to recognize the logic of ethnification at work in the rise of contextual theologies, especially in those contextual theologies that have stressed culture. One can see this in the debates in Africa as to whether cultural reconstruction as a basis for theological construction should look back to the villages or ahead to the cities.[32] While the logic of ethnification will continue to drive contextual theologies as we have known them, these theologies will have to take larger forces more into account as they continue to develop.

Primitivism

The third type of cultural logic is primitivism, which may be defined as an attempt to go back to an earlier, premodern period to find a frame of reference and meaning in order to engage the present. Just where that period is located in history, and how well it might be reconstructed in the present, is always a point of contention. Primitivism (Friedman's term) might also be called "revitalization," that is, a use of an earlier period of history to give focus and direction to the present. The period chosen is one that represents cultural or social identity at its strongest or its purest. For the Protestant Reformation and for Roman Catholic religious orders, such a period was often the "primitive Church." For much of nineteenth- and early twentieth-century Catholicism, it was the High Middle Ages.

Friedman distinguishes between cultural and natural primitivism. One can see both varieties in theology. Examples just given are instances of the former: a given cultural (theological) epoch is held up for emulation. Natural primitivisms are calls to return to nature from the corrupting influences of culture. The religious practices of the Desert Fathers were one of the earliest examples of this. Attempts to recreate pre-Christian European religion, or the worship of the proto-European goddess in some feminist and ecological circles would be examples of natural primitivisms. Primitivism differs from antiglobalism in that it is more holistic in its approach to what it wishes to retrieve. But, in any case, it calls for some invention of a tradition.

---

[32]Bénézet Bujo points this out well in his *African Theology in Its Social Context* (Maryknoll, NY: Orbis Books, 1992).

THE MEANING OF CONTEXT IN A GLOBALIZED WORLD

To return now to the opening question: what has happened to the meaning of context under the impact of globalization? If contextual theologies first arose in response to the inadequacies of universalizing theologies, what do they mean today? We have explored the phenomenon of globalization, and have tried to map a number of kinds of contextual theologies, some of which may not recognize themselves as such, but appear, in global theological flows and cultural logics, to be occupying the space between the global and the local. How has context changed? I would suggest three ways in which the change is manifest.

First of all, context as a concept has become increasingly *deterritorialized*. The compression of space in globalization has been the major player in this. Boundaries today are increasingly not boundaries of territory, but boundaries of difference. These boundaries intersect and crisscross in often bewildering fashion, as is evident in much postcolonial writing, where authors discover the multiple sources of their identities.[33] Because the space along boundaries is often a space of great semiotic activity, this has importance for understanding how cultures are being reshaped and what consequences this holds for theology. Seeing boundaries as boundaries of difference rather than as simply boundaries of territory has another consequence for theology as well. Seen from a territorial center, a boundary of territory indicates where territory ends; it is a horizon. A boundary of difference highlights issues of difference rather than elements of commonality as the basis for identity. In places where identities are contested, and in situations of ethnogenesis, boundaries of difference can indicate what elements of identity will play key roles in the construction of a theology. One frequently sees this in early stages of a new contextual theology: certain elements of difference are given more salience than will be the case later on in the development of that theology.

Second, contexts are becoming *hyperdifferentiated*. The compression of time, the world of cyberspace, and the movement of peoples mean that people are now participating in different realities at the same time—there is multiple belonging. This has to be taken into account in any attempt to express identity where multiple cultures interact at the same time. Multiple belonging is behind the discourse of "multiculturalism," in which people struggle to find a way of dealing with a variety of cultures, or fragments of cultures, occupying the same space.

---

[33]See, for example, Kwame Anthony Appiah, *In My Father's House: Africa and the Philosophy of Culture* (Cambridge, MA: Harvard University Press, 1992).

Third, contexts are more clearly *hybridized*. The purity of culture was probably always more an aspiration than a reality, but in a globalized world it becomes increasingly untenable as a concept. As was seen in looking at global theological flows and cultural logics, there is intense interaction that destabilizes once tranquil conditions. Particularly in the case of the cultural logics, the response is almost inevitably hybrid. That hybridity has to be embraced more consciously in contextual theologies; we need to realize that most of our attempts to reach an ideal point will always be but approximate.

These conclusions will be taken up again in chapters 3 and 4, where concepts of culture, identity, and religious identity as they relate to theology today will be explored in more detail.

2

Intercultural Hermeneutics: Issues and Prospects

INTRODUCTION

Given the manifold cultures that are part of the world Church today, the need to understand the conditions that make communication possible in such complexity is a point hardly open to question. People have long been aware of how language differences affect communication; one only need think back to the great christological controversies of the fourth and fifth centuries to realize how language can be a barrier to as much as a vehicle for communication. In the twentieth century the effects of culture have been more clearly ascertained, and are gradually being thematized. With the attention paid both to communication itself and to hermeneutics (theory and methods of interpretation) during this same time period, the opportunity is now being presented to begin forging more consciously an intercultural hermeneutics.

Intercultural hermeneutics builds upon intercultural communication. Intercultural communication might be defined as the ability to speak and to understand across cultural boundaries. It is a matter of speaking and hearing in a situation where a common world is not shared by speaker and hearer. Intercultural hermeneutics explores the conditions that make communication possible across cultural boundaries. It also presses the questions of the nature of meaning and of truth under those circumstances. All communication is interpretation, to be sure; but hermeneutics is required to raise questions that communication by itself may be able to postpone or to ignore. And a theological hermeneutics carries with it additional commitments regarding the meaning of revelation, tradition, and Church that must be figured into the equation.

In the social science discussion of intercultural communication, English-speaking specialists make a distinction between intercultural and cross-cultural. Intercultural refers to communication across a cultural boundary. Cross-cultural refers to generalization that can be made about intercultural communication, based on the analysis of different intercultural encounters. When applied to hermeneutics, two dimensions are reflected here. Intercultural hermeneutics, narrowly understood, is concerned with the quality and integrity of the individual communication event. Cross-cultural hermeneutics is concerned with the long-term effects—on both the message and the interlocutors—of multiple communication events. Both intercultural and cross-cultural dimensions need attention. In what follows here, "intercultural" will be used to encompass both aspects, since the intercultural is the foundation for the cross-cultural.

In speaking of intercultural hermeneutics, something needs to be said about a definition of culture as well. Culture is of course a notoriously slippery concept, with no agreed upon definition. The question of culture itself will be treated in more detail in chapter 3. The definition of culture that I will be using here is a semiotic one, based on the one developed by Jens Loenhoff.[1] It views culture as having three important dimensions. First of all, culture is ideational—it provides systems or frameworks of meaning which serve both to interpret the world and to provide guidance for living in the world. Culture in this dimension embodies beliefs, values, attitudes, and rules for behavior. Second, culture is performance—rituals that bind a culture's members together to provide them with a participatory way of embodying and enacting their histories and values. Performance also encompasses embodied behaviors. Third, culture is material—the artifacts and symbolizations that become a source for identity: language, food, clothing, music, and the organization of space.

Frequently when discussion of culture takes place, especially in matters of hermeneutics, it is the ideational dimension that is emphasized to the detriment of the other two. All three need to be taken into consideration if a culture is to be understood effectively.

It was noted that this definition is a semiotic definition of culture. Without going into the details of the semiotics of culture,[2] semiotics of

---

[1]Jens Loenhoff, *Interkulturelle Verständigung. Zum Problem grenzüberschreitender Kommunikation* (Oplade: Leske und Budrich, 1992), 144.

[2]For more detail see Robert J. Schreiter, *Constructing Local Theologies* (Maryknoll, NY: Orbis Books, 1985), chapter 3; and Alex Garcia-Rivera, *St. Martin de Porres: The "Little Stories" and the Semiotics of Culture* (Maryknoll, NY: Orbis Books, 1995), chapter 3.

culture may be defined as a method by which culture is studied as a communication structure and process. It focuses on *signs* (Greek: *semeia*) that carry *messages* along the pathways (*codes*) of culture. The purpose of the circulation of those messages within culture is to create *identity*, which involves building group solidarity and incorporating new information as it comes into the culture. The intercultural hermeneutics challenge would be stated thus semiotically: how does the same *message* get communicated via different *codes*, using a mixture of *signs* from two different cultures? This will be returned to in the discussion of the interpretive event as communication event below.

The issues and prospects for intercultural hermeneutics will be explored under five headings: (1) elements that make up the intercultural hermeneutical discussion today; (2) the conditions for successful intercultural communication; (3) the interpretive event as communication event; (4) distinctive characteristics of intercultural hermeneutics in its epistemology; and (5) other hermeneutical issues.

ELEMENTS IN THE DISCUSSION
OF INTERCULTURAL HERMENEUTICS

Exploration of difference across boundaries is, of course, not something invented in the twentieth century. In the West, from the time of Herodotus onward, difference has been acknowledged and accounted for in a variety of ways. However, intercultural hermeneutics does not have a clearly discernible history as such, but draws upon at least four areas for its own reflections today.

The first of these areas is historical studies. With the increasing sense of historical consciousness that has been part of academic scholarship since the nineteenth century, what has come to be understood as cultural difference has been examined with perspectives more and more accessible for intercultural hermeneutical reflection. This is especially the case in some of the more recent historical investigations that incorporate cultural concerns from the social sciences more directly into their historical methodologies. Such an example would be James C. Russell's *The Germanization of Early Medieval Christianity*.[3] At the same time, it should be mentioned that not every comparative study of different historical epochs or places can be called intercultural. Explicit theories of culture need to be at work, and cultural issues need to be addressed.

---

[3] James C. Russell, *The Germanization of Early Medieval Christianity: A Sociohistorical Approach to Religious Transformation* (New York: Oxford University Press, 1994).

The second area contributing to intercultural hermeneutics is comparative philosophical and theological studies. The research efforts of the Gesellschaft für interkulturelle Philosophie, which has been meeting since the early 1990s, are representative of this kind of comparative work between philosophical systems (especially those of Europe and Asia) and of attempts to form thematized philosophical systems where they have heretofore not been present (as in Africa).[4] One is reminded also of the work of the Kyoto School since the 1930s, beginning with Keiji Nishitani, of engaging Western philosophy in a Japanese Buddhist context.

Similarly, there is a lively study of comparative theology, pursued especially in the United States by scholars trained in Christian as well as in Buddhist and Hindu traditions.[5] These comparative studies are primarily intertextual in nature, and raise important questions about the reading of texts and the articulation of philosophical systems. Intercultural hermeneutics and comparative studies do not coincide completely, however, inasmuch as comparative studies are more preoccupied with systems of meaning than with culture per se.

The third area is Western philosophical hermeneutics. The hermeneutical models of interpretation as conversation, developed first by Hans-Georg Gadamer and carried further into theology by David Tracy, have been quite influential in the development of intercultural hermeneutics.[6] Gadamer's proposal of understanding as a "fusion of horizons," where "horizon" might be construed as a cultural boundary, has been an especially fertile concept. More important is the reflection on the stranger and the other, begun by Max Scheler and Georg Simmel and carried forward especially by Emmanuel Levinas.[7] As intercultural hermeneutics develops, it will need to engage with Western philosophi-

---

[4]Its proceedings are published as "Studien zur interkulturellen Philosophie" (Amsterdam: Rodopi), beginning with R. A. Mall and Dieter Lohmar (eds.), *Philosophische Grundlagen der Interkulturalität*, 1993. See also Franz Wimmer, *Interkulturelle Philosophie: Geschichte und Theorie* (Vienna: Passagen, 1990).

[5]Francis X. Clooney is the leader in this. See his *Theology After Vedanta: An Experiment in Comparative Theology* (Albany, NY: SUNY Press, 1993), and *Seeing Through Texts: Doing Theology among the Srivaisnavas of South India* (Albany, NY: SUNY Press, 1996). See also his review of comparative theology literature in *Theological Studies* 56 (1995): 521-50.

[6]Hans-Georg Gadamer, *Truth and Method* (New York: Continuum, 1975); David Tracy, *Plurality and Ambiguity: Hermeneutics, Religion, Hope* (San Francisco: Harper and Row, 1987).

[7]The theological import of the reflection on the stranger has been developed especially by Theo Sundermeier. See especially his *Den Fremden verstehen. Eine praktische Hermeneutik* (Göttingen: Vandenhoeck und Ruprecht, 1996).

cal hermeneutics and the theological hermeneutics that have developed from it.[8]

The fourth area contributing to intercultural hermeneutics is work being done in the social sciences.[9] Specifically, work by communication theorists such as William Gudykunst and Stella Ting-Toomey,[10] work in what are being called indigenous psychologies (i.e., psychological categories drawn from local cultures rather than imposed from outside),[11] and in cultural anthropology[12] are contributing frameworks based on empirical research. A good deal of this empirical work will be drawn upon in what follows here. Empirical work has the advantage of the sheer concreteness that grounds the research. At the same time, there are visible shortcomings in certain social science theories, inasmuch as they are highly dependent upon psychological models developed chiefly within the context of the United States. This is less the case with the cultural anthropological literature, although it too may be beholden to certain postmodern theories about the arbitrariness of the subject and the volatility of tradition formation.

Intercultural hermeneutics has, therefore, considerable resources upon which to draw in its theory formation. Because it is still at such an early stage, a great deal of work needs to be done. In the social science research, for example, theory formation in intercultural communication began only in the late 1980s. But even these modest beginnings will be useful for intercultural theology.

---

[8]On theological hermeneutics, see Werner G. Jeanrond, *Theological Hermeneutics: Development and Significance* (New York: Crossroad, 1991); Anthony C. Thiselton, *New Horizons in Hermeneutics* (San Francisco: Zondervan, 1992).

[9]A more extensive account of this is given in Robert J. Schreiter, "Theorie und Praxis interkultureller Kommunikationskompetenz in der Theologie," in Edmund Arens (ed.), *Anerkennung der Anderen. Eine theologische Grunddimension interkultureller Kommunikation* (Freiburg: Herder, 1995), 9-30.

[10]See especially Molefe Asante and William Gudykunst (eds.), *Handbook of International and Intercultural Communication* (London: Sage, 1989); Richard Wiseman and Jolene Koester (eds.) *Intercultural Communication Competence* (London: Sage, 1993). Stella Ting-Toomey's theory of identity negotiation is included in the Wiseman and Koester volume, 72-111.

[11]See, for example, Paul Heelas and Andrew Lock (eds.), *Indigenous Psychologies: The Anthropology of the Self* (London: Academic Press, 1981).

[12]Richard Shweder, *Thinking through Cultures: Expeditions in Cultural Psychology* (Cambridge, MA: Harvard University Press, 1991) is representative of the cognitive psychology group in cultural anthropology, who look specifically at the problem of cultural boundaries. For an example in the area of intercultural identity formation, see Richard Wilson, *Maya Resurgence in Guatemala: Q'eqchi' Experiences* (Norman, OK: Oklahoma University Press, 1995).

AIMS OF INTERCULTURAL HERMENEUTICS

Under what conditions is communication across cultural boundaries to be deemed successful? Among communication theorists, the question is first framed in terms of *competence*, in the sense of being able to do something successfully based upon an adequate command of the skills and knowledge necessary. They speak of *intercultural communication competence*. The characteristics of intercultural communication competence are *effectiveness* and *appropriateness*. A communication would be considered effective when the speaker feels that it has achieved its goal; namely, that it has become lodged with the hearer on the other side of the cultural boundary in a manner recognizable to the speaker. Thus, the speaker's satisfaction with the conclusion of the communication event is a necessary (but as we shall see, not a sufficient) condition for intercultural communication competence. A communication is appropriate when it is achieved without a violation of the hearer's cultural codes. An historical example might be helpful here to illustrate appropriateness. When the Catholic cathedral in Kyoto was built in the 1950s, stained glass windows were installed. One of them depicted St. George in the act of killing the dragon. This caused an uproar, because the dragon in East Asia is not a symbol of evil, and in Japan is a symbol of the emperor. To have St. George slay the dragon in that setting was tantamount to saying that Christianity destroys Japaneseness. Different cultural codes carried the same sign (the dragon) along very different pathways.

The social science theory of competence as effectiveness and appropriateness does not in itself reach far enough for intercultural hermeneutics. Effectiveness, for example, can become very hard to ascertain, especially when the speaker does not know the hearer's culture well. Thus, earlier in the twentieth century, when a missionary couple began work in North India as evangelists, word quickly went around the village that they owned a cat. In this village, only witches kept cats, and they were used to snatch people's souls while they were sleeping. The strangers in the village therefore had to be witches. The following morning, the male missionary gathered the men of the village together and addressed them through an interpreter, not knowing about the intense discussion that had gone on the night before. The missionary announced, "I have come to win your souls for Christ!" The astonished look on the faces of the villagers assured the missionary that he had made his point effectively. The men, however, were wondering who this Christ was, and what he wanted with their souls!

What does constitute effectiveness in intercultural communication? Beyond the requirement for adequate knowledge, two other factors complicate its assessment. One factor is time. The effect of a communication is not always immediate. In the case of religious conversion, which is the goal of much religious intercultural communication, effective understanding may need time to develop and ripen over an extended period.[13] The other factor is a change of signs. A different sign may carry the message more effectively. Perhaps having St. George slay a menacing spirit of the dead (*go-ryo*) might have been more appropriate in Kyoto's cathedral.

Similarly, in intercultural theological hermeneutics, appropriateness as a nonviolation of cultural codes may be in itself an insufficient criterion. Inasmuch as Christian faith is about conversion, one might expect that some of the cultural codes will be altered. Were that not the case, would Christian faith be any more than a veneer sanctifying any and every cultural arrangement? Yet many involved in inculturation would hold that Christ is already somehow present in the culture. If that be the case, should cultural codes need to change? And if so, which ones? As can be seen, there remain substantial questions, both philosophical and theological, even after empirical research has been done and the theory has been formed out of it.

THE INTERPRETIVE EVENT AS COMMUNICATION EVENT

The complexity of the intercultural communication event and the hermeneutical issues flowing from it can be made more intelligible by looking at each part of the communication event and reflecting briefly on the hermeneutical implications. There are three basic parts of the event: the interlocutors (speaker and hearer), the context, and the message.

The interlocutors in the intercultural communication event are usually described either as speakers and hearers, or senders and receivers. The former designation has a distinctly aural cast to it; the latter has an implicit focus on the message. Speaker and hearer will be used here, despite the aural bias, since this designation connotes living persons and communities more effectively than senders and receivers.

Early research focused upon the *attitudes* of speakers and hearers. More recently the focus has shifted to their behaviors. William

---

[13]See Robert W. Hefner (ed.), *Conversion to Christianity: Historical and Anthropological Perspectives on a Great Transformation* (Berkeley: University of California Press, 1993). For an overview of the literature, see Lewis Rambo, "Current Research on Religious Conversion," *Religious Studies Review* 8 (1982): 146-59; David Snow and Richard Machalek, "The Sociology of Conversion," *Annual Review of Sociology* 10 (1984): 167-90.

Gudykunst, for example, speaks of three sets of factors that speakers and hearers employ in intercultural communication. There are *motivation* factors (such as attraction, self-conceptions, openness to new information); *knowledge* factors (such as knowledge of more than one perspective, of similarities and differences); and *skill* factors (such as an ability to empathize, tolerate ambiguity, accommodate behavior, and gather appropriate information).[14] These are factors or attitudes that enhance the likelihood of effective communication across cultural boundaries for both speaker and hearer.

Speakers and hearers may share similar attitudinal characteristics, but they have different goals in the communication event itself. The speaker is concerned with getting a message across the cultural boundary with integrity and lodging it in the world of the hearer in such a way that it will be understood. The hearer, on the other hand, is concerned with finding a place for that message within his or her own world in such a way as to enhance the hearer's identity. In doing this, the hearer looks for an analogue of the message within his or her own world and lodges the message near it. Since the worlds of the two are constructed differently, the analogue may be more apparent than real. In the example from North India given above, the appearance of the missionaries' pet cat caused the evangelistic message to be lodged near witchcraft in the hearers' world, rather than near salvation.

What is important to note here is that, whereas the speaker has a preoccupation with the *integrity* of the message in the communication event, the hearer has a preoccupation with *identity*. The missionary was concerned with his message, hoping it would have the impact that perhaps it had had on him once upon a time. The hearers in the North Indian village were concerned with the safety of their village and their way of life. Stella Ting-Toomey especially has pressed the identity issue as the key element in ascertaining the success of the intercultural communication event: intercultural communication is not just about maintaining the integrity of the message; it is also about its impact on the hearing community.[15]

A second important thing is the need for intensive dialogue to ascertain the effectiveness and appropriateness of the communication. The message cannot be considered transmitted until a good deal of

---

[14]See the table in William Gudykunst, "Toward a Theory of Effective Interpersonal and Intergroup Communication: An Anxiety/Uncertainty Management (AUM) Perspective," in Wiseman and Koester, op. cit., 38.

[15]Ting-Toomey, op. cit. See also William R. Cupach and T. Todd Imahori, "Identity Management Theory: Communication Competence in Intercultural Episodes and Relationships," in Wiseman and Koester, op. cit., 112-31.

give-and-take between hearer and speaker has occurred in a hospitable, non-dominating kind of way. Intensive dialogue and engagement are essential to intercultural communication (and therefore to its hermeneutics). The greater the difference between the cultural worlds of speaker and hearer, the more intensive and extensive this kind of exchange will have to be.

As one might surmise, in initial contact a more strongly receiver-oriented communication may be necessary. What is being learned about reception theory in hermeneutics may be helpful here. In the course of the encounter, a greater balance between speaker and hearer may be struck. For theological hermeneutics, a concentration on the receiver may be a helpful counterweight to a preoccupation with the message or with the speaker.

The second part of the communication event is the context, which includes the cultures of both speaker and hearer and the process of their encounter.

The greater familiarity the interlocutors have with all the cultures involved, the better the communication is likely to be. But while this may be an important—even indispensable—rule in concrete communities, it becomes increasingly difficult to maintain such intimate knowledge of all communities in something as extensive as world Christianity. Here cross-cultural research can be helpful in providing some larger categories which, while not fitting perfectly, do provide some orientation toward the codes at work in different cultures. For it is the encounter with differing codes, sometimes harder to puzzle out than signs as to their dynamics and meaning, that provide the major challenge within the context.

Important work in this area has been done by the Dutch sociologist Geert Hofstede, in a study of communication characteristics in forty countries. His work has been expanded even further by a team of American researchers.[16] Hofstede established a series of scales that function roughly as what here are being called codes. A look at three of them would be illustrative of how contexts and their codes operate in the intercultural communication event.

The first of the scales is a continuum of individualist-collectivist codes. Individualist cultures prize the individual above the group, whereas collectivist cultures always locate the individual within the context of the group. The Cartesian "I think, therefore I am" versus the

---

[16]Geert Hofstede, *Culture's Consequences* (London: Sage, 1980). The scope of the study has been amplified by Michael Hecht, Peter Andersen, and Sidney Ribeau, "The Cultural Dimensions of Nonverbal Communication," in Asante and Gudykunst, op. cit., 163-85.

African "I am because we are" illustrates the difference between the individualist and collectivist positions. This difference gets played out in the codes governing proper communication and what counts for a satisfying (i.e., effective and appropriate) outcome. A member of an individualist culture feels happy with an intercultural communication event if openness and creativity have been displayed, novelty has been introduced, the individual has been left unencumbered, and the autonomy of the individual has been affirmed. Members of a collectivist culture, on the other hand, would see "openness and creativity" as a potential deviation and a lack of group solidarity. Innovation of any type needs to be seen as either a rediscovery or a reaffirmation of the group's knowledge, ethos, and solidarity. Hence, collectivist cultures prize the enrichment of new information in a way that is different from that of their individualist counterparts. New information is just a way of saying something we already know.

A second scale Hofstede proposes is low-context/high-context. In cultures with low-context codes, the influence of historical background, the knowledge of local ethos, the significance of body language and other nonverbal communication are minimized. All important contextual data are incorporated into the communication event itself. Individualist cultures, because of their emphasis on the autonomy of the individual, are frequently low-context cultures. The ultimate example of a low-context code is a computer program: nothing is assumed and every step must be explicit. High-context cultures, on the other hand, require extensive knowledge of the historical background and ethos of the community in order to understand communications. Nonverbal communication may be minimal, but it is redolent with meaning. Important information may be conveyed in ambiguous proverbs or oblique historical allusions. The use of ideograms to convey meaning in writing, as in China and Japan, is characteristic of high-context culture, as is the use of silence as a form of communication in Native American communities.

One can see the communication problems that might arise between representatives of low-context and high-context cultures. Low-context interlocutors find those from high-context cultures vague, elusive, and inexpressive. High-context interlocutors find those from low-context settings who need to spell out everything and be very direct as somewhat boorish, indicative of an uncultivated spirit. The only people to whom one must explain everything (for denizens of high-context cultures) are children, strangers, and fools.

A third scale is the tolerance of ambiguity. Ambiguity has to do with the amount of explicitation and explanation needed in any situation. Both what constitutes ambiguity itself (think of what the difference would be in high-context and low-context settings!), and where it might occur will differ. On the whole, a greater tolerance for ambiguity makes for easier intercultural communication. At any rate, attending to one's own and to others' tolerance levels is important for intercultural communication.

As was already noted above, codes provide a considerable challenge for intercultural hermeneutics, since their apparent incompatibility often lies at the heart of communication difficulty. Particularly those codes that create the conditions of possibility for communication (e.g., how one is to conduct oneself in conversation, who may talk to whom, what counts for politeness and rudeness) pose special difficulty.

The third part of the communication event is the message. Following the tripartite definition of culture proposed above (ideational, performantial, material), messages are embedded in all three dimensions. For example, the central message of Christianity about the passion, death, and resurrection of Jesus Christ is formulated and transmitted in words (the Bible, creeds, doctrines, catechisms), in acts (the liturgical drama of Holy Week), and in signs (the cross). Here is where a semiotics of culture can be useful to intercultural communication: messages are not seen as being restricted to verbal or print media.

An important principle in interpersonal (and a fortiori, intercultural) communication is of special significance when considering the message. It has to do with the transmission of information. Information is both lost and gained when crossing a cultural boundary. Aspects of a message that are obvious and transparent in the speaker's culture may become obscure and opaque in the hearer's culture. Hence, information is "lost" to the hearer (lost in the sense of not immediately understood, though potentially retrievable at a later time). An example is the transition Christianity made from a predominantly Jewish culture to a Hellenistic one. The angel-christologies of Jewish Christianity, for example, disappear for all practical purposes as christology takes on other issues and other forms. Interestingly, they are reappearing in African and Mesoamerican christologies today.[17] This is an example of a loss of information later retrieved.

But even with this loss, the encounter with Hellenistic culture provided gains. Would the *homoousios* formula have been possible within a predominantly Jewish cultural framework? The pattern of loss and

[17]Fergus King, "Angels and Ancestors: A Basis for Christology?" *Mission Studies* 11 (1994): 27-42 explores this for Africa. For a similar account in two Mayan peoples, see Manuel Marzal et al. (eds.), *El rostro indio de Dios* (Lima: Pontificia Universidad Catolica de Peru, 1991) (English translation, *The Indian Face of God in Latin America* [Maryknoll, NY: Orbis Books, 1996]).

gain of information might provide another way of exploring the meaning of the development of dogma, with the crossing of the cultural boundary being seen not as imparting new information, but of drawing out or summoning forth the implications of belief. Needless to say, the latter approach would likely be preferred in any event by a collectivist culture.

As is evident in these few illustrations, analysis of the intercultural communication event from the perspective of communication theory evokes a number of hermeneutical issues, both philosophical and theological. Some of these will be returned to below.

INTERCULTURAL HERMENEUTICS IN ITS EPISTEMOLOGY

Now that we have looked at the intercultural communication event and some of the hermeneutical issues it raises, we may find it worthwhile to look briefly at some of the distinctive characteristics of this hermeneutics vis-à-vis other hermeneutical positions. Specifically, four distinctive characteristics will be noted, relating to meaning, truth, sameness/difference, and agency.

MEANING

Following Paul Ricoeur, one can situate meaning as it relates to a text (using "text" here in the broader sense of the term). Does it lie behind the text (in the mind of the author, as in Romantic hermeneutics)? In that instance, knowing the intention of the author is key to understanding the text. Or does meaning lie in the text itself, as structuralist and some postmodern readings would say? Then one must plumb the structures of the text to understand its meaning. Or is meaning in front of the text, in the interaction between text and reader? Then one must investigate the reception of the text and the reaction of the reader.

Does intercultural hermeneutics press us in any specific direction in this scheme of reading? One could opine that individualist cultures might prefer the Romantic reading, while those from collectivist cultures, where individual authorship often remains submerged in the group, would opt for finding meaning in the text. Cultures that place strong emphasis on performance (for example, primarily oral cultures where there is little private reading) might choose the third possibility. Thus specific cultures may, internally, privilege one reading over the others.

If one uses the elements of the intercultural communication event just described, one might look at the question of meaning as follows. Does meaning lie with the speaker? At least initially, one might hold that such would be the case, insofar as the speaker initiates the message. But in the explorations of effectiveness and appropriateness above, it was clear that the speaker cannot achieve or assure communication without the hearer and an intensive dialogue process. In the case of the missionary in the village in India, he was sure of the meaning of the message, but its meaning was lost on his hearers.

So does meaning lie with the hearers (Ricoeur's third possibility)? For much the same reason as just given for the speaker, this is no guarantee. The hearers may not have the appropriate framework to hear the message. One is reminded of Paul's speech at the Areopagus in Acts 17. His hearers had no way of taking talk of resurrection from the dead seriously.

Does meaning reside then in the text itself? Because texts can carry multiple meanings, one cannot establish this claim as a criterion in itself, even with texts held as divinely inspired. Take for example the case of the Buddhist university student who, upon reading the four Gospels followed by the Acts of the Apostles, thought that the Gospels narrated not four versions of the life of Jesus, but four incarnations of Jesus on the way to Enlightenment (which is what he took the story of the Ascension at the beginning of the Acts of the Apostles to mean). In each of the four Gospels, after all, Jesus is born and then dies. The last of the Gospels presents Jesus in a far more spiritual light, indicating his imminent entry into Nirvana. The *jataka* tales (tales of previous lives of the Buddha) are part of a familiar genre in Buddhist literature. What was awe-inspiring for the student was that it took Jesus only four lives to reach Buddhahood, and it had taken Siddhartha Gautama a thousand lives to do so.

Where, then, might meaning reside? Social science researchers suggest that it might be in what they call the "social judgment" of those involved in the intercultural communication event. Social judgment entails the interaction of all parties in establishing meaning. No single party can be assured of correct interpretation without help from the others. Meaning emerges out of the interaction. Such an understanding would seem to give some favor to meaning being in front of the text, but this may be deceptive. The interaction of the interlocutors, aware of their contexts, with the text may create a new reality.

Fumitaka Matsuoka alludes to something like this when he proposes that speakers and hearers do not come together in the culture of each other, but in an interstitial zone created out of the liminal experience of both interlocutors interacting with each other. He suggests that it is perhaps in this specially created zone that intercultural communication takes place.[18]

Matsuoka's proposal seems to respect the etic or outsider quality of much intercultural communication, in which we try to represent ourselves to our hearers in ways that they will understand. Both interlocutors may end up doing this, creating antechambers to their respective cultures, as it were, into which they bring what others might understand, and into which others are invited. Entry into the Holy of Holies of the culture may be precluded until longer contact has taken place.[19]

Matsuoka's proposal may be particularly helpful in encounters of highly incommensurate cultures, of cultures that have been damaged badly by outside invaders, and of cultures that maintain a kind of *disciplina arcani*. An interstitial zone may protect important aspects of the culture's life. In any event, the proposal is also helpful in reminding us of the importance of finding ways to *imagine* the cultural encounter.

TRUTH

A second distinctive characteristic of intercultural hermeneutics is its concept of truth. This follows on its understanding of meaning as social judgment, and what has been said about the maintenance of identity in the intercultural communication event. In the West, truth claims are adjudicated by recasting the truth questions in propositional forms. Intercultural hermeneutics seems to suggest that approaches based on such propositional and referential notions of truth do not reach far enough. It has been noted that, alongside the integrity of the message, the identity of the hearers or the hearing community also has to be taken into account. So understood, truth may not be able to be extracted propositionally as a way of arriving at truth-claim candidates. Truth is embedded in the narratives of living communities. As was noted in the beginning of chapter 1, the valuing of abstract truth over embedded truth has a context and a history in European modernity. Descartes' search for the abstract provided a way of rising above the

---

[18]Fumitaka Matsuoka, "A Reflection on 'Teaching Theology from an Intercultural Perspective,'" *Theological Education* 36, no. 1 (1989): 35-42. In a similar vein, following anthropologist Paul Rabinow, Mark Taylor, "In Praise of Shaky Ground: The Liminal Christ and Cultural Pluralism," *Theology Today* 43 (1987): 36-51.

[19]Here the work that continues to be done on Kenneth Pike's proposal about emic and etic approaches to culture (roughly, insider and outsider) may prove useful. See Thomas N. Headland, Kenneth L. Pike and Marvin Harris (eds.), *Emics and Etics: The Insider/Outsider Debate* (London: Sage, 1990).

deadly doctrinal confrontations of the Thirty Years' War. The West's commitment to technical rationality only strengthens its commitment to propositional truth.

For much of the world, however, such representations of truth appear pallid. One needs something closer to what has been called in the West existential truth. Here, keeping to the tripartite understanding of culture proposed above can be a useful way to avoid overemphasizing the ideational at the cost of the performantial and material. Identity—and truth—are embedded in all three (just as falsehood can be). Propositional truth might be seen as a necessary but not sufficient condition for establishing intercultural truth. Many peoples of the world have that sense already. They will not believe what strangers say until they see how strangers live.

The adjudication of truth is not only one of the most difficult areas in intercultural hermeneutics, but also one of the most crucial. It will have to take into account the multivalent aspects of meaning just discussed, and insist that it is not just a problem caused by intercultural difference (which would reduce it to a problem of technical rationality), but calls for a different way of approaching the question at all.[20]

BALANCING DIFFERENCE AND SAMENESS

A third characteristic of intercultural hermeneutics is its way of balancing difference and sameness between the aims of intercultural and cross-cultural hermeneutics. That balance is not a perfect or complete one; it is constantly under negotiation. Intercultural hermeneutics (narrowly understood) is concerned with cultural distinctiveness or difference, with how meaning will negotiate a cultural boundary. It is wary of homogenization. It resists easy absorption or assimilation. Cross-cultural hermeneutics, on the other hand, seeks those forms of sameness that will allow easier communication in a world with so many cultures. Consequently, it seeks commonalities or at least common categories that will promote communication and understanding. Put another way, this involves bringing together, from an epistemological point of view, emic (insider) and etic (outsider) distinctions, respecting the view of culture that each culture has of itself, yet finding a way to speak authentically across a range of cultures—what Heelas and Lock have called a "derived etic."[21]

---

[20]For an account of the struggles involved, see Thomas Dean (ed.), *Religious Pluralism and Truth: Essays on Cross-Cultural Philosophy of Religion* (Albany, NY: SUNY Press, 1995).

[21]Heelas and Lock, op. cit., Introduction.

Balancing difference and sameness has ethical as well as epistemological significance. Denial of difference can lead to the colonization of a culture and its imagination. Denial of similarities promotes an anomic situation where no dialogue appears possible and only power will prevail.

In addition to epistemological and ethical aspects, this question has theological dimensions also. Two can be named here. First of all, what is the theological significance of difference? Are we to understand difference in God's creation as merely decorative or is it somehow revelatory? Is the plenitude of difference simply a display of God's power or does it tell us something about being itself? We need a much more profound and thoroughgoing theology of culture and of grace in order to be able to probe that question.[22]

Second, in a globalizing world that cannot thematize its own *telos*, that is, cannot imagine a goal beyond its own ideals of progress, equality, and inclusion, what cross-cultural elements emerge from the worldwide Christian experience that might provide a coherent vision of the future? The global theological flows of liberation, feminism, ecology, and human rights represent one set of responses, addressed particularly to the contradictions and failures of globalization. The cultural logics of antiglobalism, ethnification, and primitivism protest the failures of globalization and offer alternative, though limited, visions of what might be achieved, usually based on some reimagining of the past. What needs to be developed is a cross-cultural view of the human, a new theological anthropology. In the final chapter, I will propose that an overarching category may be reconciliation, with catholicity as the means of expressing it.

AGENCY

A fourth epistemological characteristic of intercultural hermeneutics is its emphasis on agency. There can be no passive or inert players in the intercultural communication event, no subjects robbed of their subjectivity. In too much reflection on intercultural dynamics in Christian evangelization, there is an overemphasis on whether "they" (the hearers) are going to get the Christian message right, or whether "syncretism" is creeping in. There is not enough emphasis on the transformation of the speaker—the experience of being evangelized by the poor spoken of by liberation theologians, or the conversion of the evangelizer spoken of by Paul VI.[23] A healthy sense of agency is needed.

---

[22]See in this regard Stephen Webb, *The Gifting God: A Trinitarian Ethics of Excess* (Oxford: Oxford University Press, 1996).

[23]Paul VI, Apostolic Exhortation *Evangelii nuntiandi*, 15.

Cultural transmission does not happen mechanically, nor is it received passively. This is a theme to which we shall return in chapter 4.

Meaning, truth, difference and sameness, agency—these are four areas where intercultural hermeneutics touches basic epistemological issues and begins to define itself. That process of definition raises theological issues as well.

FURTHER ISSUES

A good number of theoretical issues have already been raised for intercultural hermeneutics, but three more need to be noted briefly.

The first is the role of power in the formation of knowledge. Since the groundbreaking work of Michel Foucault it has become commonplace to search out the machinations of power in the production and representation of knowledge.[24] This search is of particular importance to intercultural encounter because power distorts so much intercultural communication. Under the influence of Foucault and other masters of hermeneutic suspicion we now have available more and more detailed studies of how power has distorted intercultural communication, especially in creating what Serge Gruzinski has called "la colonisation de l'imaginaire,"[25] the destruction and replacement of a way of being and life by powerful invaders, and the struggle of the conquered people to maintain themselves and their identities, often in a subaltern fashion. Some of this will be explored in the next two chapters.

But we also need to examine the other side of power: how power can be mobilized across cultural boundaries. This is necessary not only to understanding the basic "puissance" behind both mass and tribal movements today,[26] but also to discovering how the religious performances (in Beyer's sense of the term) of antisystemic global movements can bring about change in the macrostructures of society. It is clear that communities can be so organized. How is it done, and can it be done on the macro level?

The second issue, that of conversion, was alluded to briefly earlier. As was noted, there is a growing literature exploring how conversion

---

[24] Michel Foucault, *Power/Knowledge* (New York: Pantheon, 1980) is one of the more accessible entry points to Foucault's ideas.

[25] Serge Gruzinski, *La Colonisation de l'imaginaire: Societés indigènes et occidentalisation dans le Mexique espagnol XVIe-XVIIIe siècle* (Paris: Gallimard, 1987). English translation, *The Conquest of Mexico* (Cambridge: Polity, 1993).

[26] The term is Michel Maffesoli's, used to designate the basic drive that spurs communities into action. See his *The Time of the Tribes* (London: Sage, 1996).

does (and does not) take place. Conversion is key to understanding Panikkar's intercultural hermeneutics and David Krieger's proposal for a new universalism.[27] Conversion has been called "learning a second first language"—learning a new way of seeing and being in the world in the same manner as that in which we learned our first language. Conversion is a term frequently invoked in global theological flows and in the language of intercultural encounter. How might what we are finding out about conversion clarify the learning process in intercultural hermeneutics?

The third issue reflects the second and also the discussion of difference and sameness above: the relative incommensurability of cultures. To hold that cultures are utterly incommensurate would mean there is no common humanity, something that is not a tenable position, at least for Christians. Yet difference needs to be respected.[28] What can be learned about an "anthropology of incommensurability," as Mario Biagioli has called it,[29] not simply in a glib postmodern fashion, but so as to understand difference in such a way that it is neither homogenized nor isolated? What will this mean for a Christian understanding of difference?

As was noted at the beginning of this chapter, the creation of an intercultural hermeneutics is still at its beginnings. But to live in a globalized world requires that we find much more routinized ways of coming to intercultural understanding. The tribalism that has grown increasingly strong in the 1990s, a tribalism based on an explicit strategy not to communicate, will be lethal if it is not countered. To mobilize good, to come to a vision of a new humanity, to approach some level of reconciliation makes the elaboration of such a hermeneutics utterly necessary.

---

[27]Raimundo Panikkar, *The Intrareligious Dialogue* (New York: Paulist Press, 1978); idem, *Myth, Faith, and Hermeneutics* (New York: Paulist Press, 1979). David Krieger, *The New Universalism: Foundations for a Global Theology* (Maryknoll, NY: Orbis Books, 1991).

[28]See Sanford Budick and Wolfgang Iser (eds.), *The Translatability of Cultures: Figurations of the Space Between* (Stanford: Stanford University Press, 1996), especially the essay by Jan Assmann.

[29]Mario Biagioli, *Galileo Courtier: The Practice of Science in the Age of Absolutism* (Chicago: University of Chicago Press, 1993), 211-44.

3

Changing Concepts of Culture and Intercultural Theology

INTRODUCTION

The previous two chapters have tried to set the stage for under-standing local theologies today. The first chapter proposed a way of looking at the contemporary world through the lens of the globalization process. Through that lens one is able to situate different contextual theologies, using the concepts of global theological flows and cultural logics. Because of globalizing processes today, what constitutes the contexts for theology is also changing. The compression of time and space means that territory becomes in many instances a less useful or-ganizing concept than in the past. Boundaries of territory are replaced by boundaries of difference. The intensity of intercultural contact not only heightens the sense of difference, but also leads to a greater need to differentiate, to account for difference. Those differentiations then combine and recombine in processes of hybridization. All of this is to say that context and culture are complexified as people experience be-longing in multiple contexts (or conversely, not belonging anywhere), and find themselves struggling to negotiate their place in the world.

In the second chapter, we explored the special qualities of commu-nication and interpretation in such an environment. Understandings of meaning, truth, difference and sameness, and agency were presented, as well as distinctive aspects of the intercultural communication event itself.

The next step in understanding what is happening in theology today is to look at the concept of culture itself. From what was said about the globalization process, it is evident that the concept of culture is undergoing change. Inasmuch as culture plays a significant role in theology (to the extent that all theologies are somehow local theologies), it becomes important to track how concepts of culture are changing, and what impact that might have on the directions theologies are taking today.

As is well known, there is no definition of culture that is widely agreed upon. This is due in part to the sheer complexity with which human communities surround themselves. In recent years culture has been compared to computer software—seemingly infinitely adaptable and inventive, driving the hardware of our bodies and physical environments, creating new possibilities.

But the inability to define culture is also due in part to the fact that we come to culture with such different questions and interests. And as we do so—looking for material causes, social processes, patterns of domination and hegemony, or webs of meaning—we pursue methods that take us to our goal, reconfiguring the roadmap along the way. Cultures appear to be infinitely malleable, amenable to so many different interpretations. We think that we have captured them in one shape, only to have them metamorphose into another.

At the beginning of chapter 2, a brief definition of culture was proposed, emphasizing that culture consists of ideas and rules, performance, and material artifacts. The method proposed for understanding culture was a semiotic one, looking especially at how signs carry messages through a culture, creating the circulation of meaning.[1] Rather than refine the definition, let it remain in the background as a general principle during the presentation in this chapter. A tighter definition of culture, at this stage, will likely not help sort through the complexities.

In this chapter, we examine two sets of concepts of culture. The first set might be called integrated concepts,[2] and the second, globalized concepts. The genesis of each will be discussed, followed by some assessment of their strengths and weaknesses. This will then allow us to move into discussion of their relative value for constructing and interpreting local theology today.

INTEGRATED CONCEPTS OF CULTURE

Integrated concepts of culture depict culture as patterned systems in which the various elements are coordinated in such a fashion as to

---

[1] See note 1 in chapter 2, above.

[2] The term is drawn from Margaret S. Archer's discussion of what she calls the "myth of cultural integration" in her *Culture and Agency: The Place of Culture in Social Theory* (Cambridge: Cambridge University Press, 1989), 1-21.

create a unified whole. The patterned nature provides a sense of recurrence and sameness that gives to those who participate in the culture a certain identity (the etymological root of which is "same"). The familiarity of the patterns offers a sense of security and of being "at home." The coordination of the different patterned systems gives rise to a sense of organic connection among the parts.

The model of such an integrated concept of culture is the traditional society, relatively self-enclosed and self-sufficient, and governed by a rule-bound tradition. Such societies are small-scale, characteristic of the *Gemeinschaft*, with face-to-face relations being the principal form of interaction.

This integrated concept of culture has dominated anthropological writing since the inception of that discipline in the nineteenth century. It has also been influential in sociology as well, providing the framework for functionalism in both disciplines. In American sociology it was particularly evident in the work of Pitrim Sorokin and Talcott Parsons.

Much of its credibility comes from the common-sense experience of living in one's own culture. If one's experience of one's own culture is one of security and meaningfulness, then the various things that make up the culture—ideas, rules, values, rituals, material artifacts—seem to fit together: they make sense. One is not drawn into fundamental questioning of the assumptions upon which the culture is based. This corresponds to the experience of those who have lived fairly contented lives in their culture, and have not ventured out beyond that culture.

Such an integrated concept has no doubt been reinforced by ethnographic studies that have focused their inquiry upon small-scale, rural societies. Such studies, as studies, needed to be circumscribed and manageable (often as the bases of doctoral dissertations), but that very approach may have also given rise to the phenomenon they purported to study.

The origins of the integrated concept of culture are usually traced back to Johann Gottfried Herder's *Outline of a Philosophy of the History of Man* and other writings, although his thought was anticipated already in Giambattista Vico's *Scienza Nuova*.[3] In Robert J. C. Young's artful reading of Herder, he proposes that Herder is both within the Enlightenment and in the Romantic reaction against it. As someone committed to the Enlightenment, he wanted to preserve a concept of the

---

[3]Herder's writings on this subject are collected in F. M. Barnard (ed.), *J. G. Herder on Social and Political Culture* (Cambridge: Cambridge University Press, 1969). Vico's work was translated by T. C. Bergin and M. H. Fisch as *The New Science of Giambattista Vico* (Ithaca, NY: Cornell University Press, 1948). See also Isaiah Berlin, *Vico and Herder: Two Studies in the History of Ideas* (New York: Viking Press, 1976).

unity of humankind, with each society contributing to the totality of humanity. He was thus quite against any European ethnocentrism that would have denigrated the quality of non-European cultures. He wished to maintain the integrity of each people's way of life. Despite much late-twentieth-century rhetoric, there was a great deal of critique of Eurocentrism in the eighteenth-century Enlightenment, as Tzvetan Todorov has pointed out.[4] But Herder is perhaps best known for his Romantic reading of human societies. In protest against the universalizing tendencies of the French Enlightenment, Herder stressed that human societies were organic unities, where land, language, and tradition came together to produce a single, irreplaceable spirit. Such a view of a *Volk* in its tradition-governed totality stood against the encroachments of progress hailed by the Enlightenment. Herder's view is tinged by not a little nostalgia for a time he felt was passing and for an imagined past. In Romantic thought these organic societies were held up as alternatives to the Enlightenment ideal. Because of their close attachment to a specific territory, they were considered to be more "natural." With the publication of E. B. Tylor's *Primitive Culture* in 1871, the organic perspective helped define the "primitive" in ethnography, a concept that has stalked anthropology down to the present time.[5]

The influence of the integrated concept of culture can be seen in theology as well. Much of the pressure for developing contextual theologies has presumed the distinctiveness and relative boundedness of culture, implying thereby that distinctive theologies could be formed. Such theologies share Romanticism's reaction to universalizing tendencies, be they modernizing, Westernizing, or colonizing in nature. In the Roman Catholic Church, papal and Vatican documents, with their positive view of culture as shaper of humanity, seem to imply an integrated concept of culture as well.

STRENGTHS OF INTEGRATED CONCEPTS OF CULTURE

The integrated concept of culture has much to commend it. The idea of a patterned, integrated whole in which one struggles to achieve an ever greater organic unity serves as a firm base for values that most would want to uphold. Culture's integrating, centripetal tendency be-

---

[4]Tzvetan Todorov, *Nous et les autres: La Reflexion francaise sur la diversité humaine* (Paris: Seuil, 1989). See Robert J. C. Young's masterful overview of the period in his *Colonial Desire: Hybridity in Theory, Culture and Race* (London: Routledge, 1995), 29-54.

[5]Edward Burnett Tylor, *Primitive Culture: Researches into the Development of Mythology, Philosophy, Art, and Custom* (New York: Harper, 1958).

speaks a certain holism that stands against the fragmentation of mass society. The relatedness of its parts evokes an image of communion, bringing a sense of coherence to the diverse elements which make it up. The concerted and conscious efforts to achieve integration speak of a positive agency of the members of that culture, making themselves into fully developed human beings.

Such a concept of culture also seems to fall in line with cumulative, conjunctive ways of thinking. In "both-and" ways of thinking (as contrasted with disjunctive, or "either-or" ways of thinking), knowledge is arrived at not through ever greater analysis, picking and paring away more and more of the idea until the core is revealed, but by a careful ordering and balancing of things until nothing is left out. Wisdom is valued above analysis. Harmony is sought, rather than differentiation. Such ways of thinking are prevalent in many oral cultures (where knowledge pared away in analysis is lost knowledge), and in many Asian cultures. Because such ways of thinking are so prevalent among so many cultures around the world, it makes sense to thematize these cultures with a concept of culture in the same cumulative, conjunctive mode.

Finally, integrated concepts of culture may be seen as a protest against the more corrosive aspects of modernity and the capitalism that fuels it. Both progress and profit require asymmetries to spark creativity in order that there might be new possibilities and new markets. Such asymmetries in power and distribution of goods are destabilizing at best and violent at worst. Much of the trenchant criticism of modernity and capitalism has been aimed at the destabilizing, and frequently dehumanizing, presupposition of asymmetry at the basis of the notion of progress. The integrated concepts of culture, by emphasizing unity and harmony, go against the competitive pressure and the fragmenting tendency of capitalism.

WEAKNESSES OF INTEGRATED CONCEPTS OF CULTURE

Were these positive characteristics of integrated concepts of culture the only things that could be said about them, then they would probably be considered beyond critique. But there are negative aspects to what Margaret S. Archer has called "the myth of cultural integration."[6] She finds such concepts hopelessly vague despite the importance accorded to them; they are more aesthetic than analytic in quality. As a result, culture becomes a loose cannon on the deck of sociology, playing "the most wildly vacillating role.... Hence, in various sociological theories, culture swings from being the prime mover (credited with en-

---

[6]Archer, op. cit., 6.

gulfing and orchestrating the entire social structure) to the opposite extreme where it is reduced to a mere epiphenomenon (charged only with providing an ideational representation of structure)."[7] She argues that the premise of integration obscures cultural dynamics and their interaction with other systems within society.

Other criticisms have also been raised. The integrating tendency of such concepts of culture can become static and fixated at best, and totalizing and essentializing at worst. They exclude or suppress that which cannot be assimilated and integrated into the whole. Discourses of protest in liberationist, feminist, and postcolonial theory have made this criticism almost commonplace today, and much historical analysis has tried to retrieve what had not been integrated. In a time when pluralism is more widely assumed, such absorptive strategies of integrated concepts of culture cannot be justified. Totalizing approaches muffle the voices of the dissident and the minority, and of those who find no home in the integrated whole. People who are immigrants, such as refugees, or who are oppressed do not experience their culture as integrated; indeed, the opposite is the case. It is experienced as fragmented. And minority culture groups must also live constantly with the larger, more powerful culture.

Integrated concepts of culture can also essentialize, that is, give the impression of more solidity than is actually the case. Archer cites as an example the well-known work of British anthropologist E. E. Evans-Pritchard on the Azande of East Africa. His work has been considered exemplary of how to view cultures as an integrated whole. However, at one point late in his career, he looked back on Zande culture as "a thing of shreds and patches." Archer goes on to quote Ernest Gellner, who found it

> ironical that this culture of shreds and patches, incorporating at least 20 culturally alien groups and speaking at least 8 languages in what is but part of its total territory, should have come to have been systematically invoked ... as an illustration of the quite erroneous view that cultures are islands to themselves, whose supposed coherent internal norms of what is real and what is not real may not be challenged.[8]

As shall be seen below, reaction against essentializing tendencies in integrated concepts of culture has prompted some authors to go to the other extreme, either finding no coherence at all, or seeing any coherence as hegemony.

---

[7]Ibid., 1.
[8]Ibid., 8.

Among the positive aspects of integrated concepts of culture, their ability to focus attention on the specificity of cultures is certainly among the most attractive. Cultures are thus able to be profiled in their distinctiveness and integrity, something that is indispensable for any discourse of difference. In his review of the influence of Herder's discourse of difference in the nineteenth century, Young points out that discourses of difference fell all too easily into racist discourses. A politics of difference presupposes a sameness and equality among cultures, although this remains an indeterminate postulate, since the nature of the sameness and equality is not specified. Remove that postulate, and one has license to treat cultures deemed inferior with something less than respect.[9] The indeterminate character of the postulate can have another effect as well. It can permit a slide into a relativism that ends up being indifferent to difference, undermining the difference of culture from the other side.

Finally, integrated concepts of culture may be no more than a generalizing gaze upon the other. Ethnographers, tiring of the chaos of their own culture, may project order on the cultures they do not know. The same may occur out of a nostalgia for a simpler, premodern time. Or the generalization about what is not known is a foregoing of examination in closer detail. In all of these instances, a naive or dismissive understanding of another culture ("it must be simpler than our culture because it is less developed") may see more order in another culture than can be discerned in one's own.

As can be seen from this brief assessment, there are both positive and negative aspects of integrated concepts of culture. With the defenders of such concepts, we can say that it is not surprising that people try to discern and establish order in their culture, much as they do in their own lives. With the opponents of such concepts, we can remind ourselves that cultures are never as unified as the models that try to explain them. Standing between these positions, we can see how integrated concepts are part of a quest for order and understanding. And perhaps because of this quest, they will not account for conflict and change very well.

INTEGRATED CONCEPTS OF CULTURE AND THEOLOGY

If one turns to theology that works with integrated concepts of culture, one sees some of the same strengths and weaknesses. As was already noted, many contextual theologies and church documents on culture either imply or directly use integrated concepts of culture. This

---

[9]Young, op. cit., 50.

should not be surprising in a religious tradition that values unity and communion, and that professes holism in its concern for the human community. Such concepts are especially attractive when religion is understood as a quest for meaning and for the design of God in the world; one becomes inclined to find the order one seeks. By including the modern (which means the integrated) concept of culture in its understanding of the human, the Roman Catholic Church since the Second Vatican Council has been able to emphasize the dignity of cultures, the role of culture in bringing human beings to their fulfillment, and the right of a people to their own culture. All of these commitments imply some integrated concept of culture.[10] The concern for the evangelization of cultures that has so marked the pontificate of John Paul II, with its implied optimism about the human ability to change a culture, would imply a belief in its patterned character.

But theologies based on such concepts of culture are likely to suffer from some of the weaknesses of these concepts as well. Most visibly, they will be able to deal better with issues of cultural identity than with the challenges of social change—just as integrated concepts of culture work more readily with patterns of culture than with cultural change that defies integration. A second area where the weakness shows is in conceptualizing the relation between faith and culture. How might Christian faith be inculturated in a new context without displacing some (integrating) aspect of that culture altogether? The culture of the evangelizer is often so closely identified with faith itself that the two become inseparable. When that happens, the culture being evangelized is displaced or destroyed. One has to become Western in order to become Christian. A third area, to which we will turn in the next chapter, is that of syncretism. Does not the use of the term syncretism imply the disturbing of some unity? And is perhaps the intractability of the syncretism issue not tied up with how we conceive of culture and identity in the first place?

GLOBALIZED CONCEPTS OF CULTURE

Partly due to the inherent weaknesses in integrated concepts of culture, and partly due to the changing contexts in the world under the influence of changes in the late twentieth century, alternative readings of culture have emerged. I am calling them here globalized concepts of culture, since they reflect the tensions and pressures arising out of the

[10]See the studies in Joseph Gremillion (ed.), *The Church and Culture since Vatican II* (Notre Dame, IN: University of Notre Dame Press, 1985).

globalization process. These concepts are found especially in postcolonial writing and in the literature of globalization. They represent two different, but related concepts of culture in a globalized world.

In postcolonial theory culture is not understood in terms of ideas and objects, but principally as a ground of contest in relations. Notions of power tend to disappear behind the curtain in integrated concepts of culture, but in globalized concepts power is foregrounded. Culture is something to be constructed rather than discovered, and it is constructed on the stage of struggle amid the asymmetries of power. It is mapped out on the axes of sameness and difference, comparability and incommensurability, cohesion and dispersion, collaboration and resistance. Diversity is prized, but difference is valued even more highly. Culture, especially from the perspective of minority groups and the colonized, disrupts the homogeneous narratives of the powerful. This is accomplished through disrupting the smooth relationships between meaning and reference, shattering the mirror of representation to show that things are really not what they seem to be. Culture in this sense strives to establish a "third space" between self and other, beyond colonizer and colonized.[11] Identity too is a concern in globalized concepts of culture, but identity is always viewed as fragmentary or multiple, constructed and imagined.

The globalization process, presented in the first chapter, provides another set of concepts of culture. Through the networks of communication, symbols and patterns are circulated through various regions and through the whole world itself. To be sure, they are received differently in various regions, and their actual context may be recrafted to accommodate certain cultural niches. These cultural flows, to use Paul Gilroy's term, may inform global systems or the antisystemic movements that attempt to counter them. They provide codes such as that of the rock concert that is understood as a form worldwide and has been artfully adapted by John Paul II for papal masses. Rap music, MTV, video art, American fast food, and athletic clothing offer a universalizing cultural discourse in which local cultures can participate in order to achieve a sense of cosmopolitan living, with the allure of a breadth of perspective and resources that seem to embrace the entire world.

These cultural flows do not constitute cultures themselves, since their play on desire requires the participants to fill in with fantasy that which is only alluded to in the cultural flow: living the life of the rock star, having rewarding experiences of family and friends when eating at McDonald's, or gaining the transcendent power of the star athlete.

---

[11] Homi K. Bhabha, *The Location of Culture* (London: Routledge, 1994), 37. Bhabha is a leading figure in postcolonial thought.

Global culture in this sense is a hyperculture or a cultural flow that moves in and out of local cultures, but is constituted as a culture itself only in the mind or in fantasy. Yet participating in the cultural flow gives those who enter the fantasy an experience of transcending their local context.[12]

The experience of globalization also unleashes a variety of cultural logics, as we saw in chapter 1. Some of these logics express themselves in antiglobalism, resisting the incursion of the global; others reassert their particularity in reacting to the universalizing thrusts of the global; and still others refashion an imagined past in their encounter with the global. The experience of the global is frequently not benign, especially in poorer countries. Global economics can commodify local markets, putting them on the roller coaster of the world market. It can encourage planting cash export crops that upset local economic ecologies, only to be followed by a crash in world prices. It can foment displacement of populations through migration of the young, undercutting any Herderian sense of the unity of place, language, and tradition. And the sudden incursion of global cultural flows may corrode local values and unravel community relationships.

Global-local encounters, then, are experienced by many in the world as uneven, asymmetrical, unequal, and violent.[13] They are experienced as disruptive, as global markets enter local cultures and rearrange their lives. They are disorienting, as people experience what Fernando Calderon has called "tiempos mixtos,"[14] a situation in which the premodern, the modern, and the postmodern exist together in the same place. Or the encounter with the global may mean the destruction of the local altogether, as local communities become migrants and refugees.

Even for those who experience globalization positively, the local encounter may bring disruption and disorientation. As Ulrich Beck has pointed out, living in postmodern society is characterized by reflexivity and risk.[15] The compression of time and space, with the presence of migrants, workers, and refugees, introduces some measure of reflexivity

---

[12]See Jonathan Friedman, *Cultural Identity and Global Process* (London: Sage, 1994), 147-66 for an account of people living out the fantasy of Parisian haut couture in Zaire.

[13]For an account of some of the interactions of the global with local culture, see Mike Featherstone, *Undoing Modernity: Globalization, Postmodernism and Identity* (London: Sage, 1995), 86-101, especially 97-99.

[14]Fernando Calderon, "America Latina, identidad y tiempos mixtos, o cómo de ser boliviano," *Imagenes desconocidas* (Buenos Aires: CLASCO, 1988), 225-29.

[15]Ulrich Beck, *Risk Society: Toward a New Modernity* (London: Sage, 1992). See also the discussion of reflexivity and risk in chapter 1.

into the lives of those who heretofore had been able to live naively in their own cultures. The heightened risks of environmental catastrophe, of employment insecurity, and the fears of crime and contamination create new anxieties, even among the wealthy. Elaborate means may be taken to insulate oneself from these risks, even to the point of building fortress-like enclaves to keep away the poor (what is being called the "Brazilianization" of cities).[16] But the awareness and the anxiety seep through nonetheless. From a religious point of view, heightened risk leads to efforts at greater contingency management, which in turn opens more windows to the transcendent, as the securities of secularization prove less reliable.

Reflexivity among those who experience globalization positively is manifested in the phenomenon of postmodernism itself. The collapse of any metanarrative that provides a public and shared grounding for society, and the proliferation of enclaves of similar thought and lifestyle, reflect the differentiation that globalization brings in its wake. The interest in communitarian philosophy in North America and Europe, a philosophy that tries to hold on to values of community and yet endorse the liberal notions of choice in a globalized society, grows out of this postmodern reflexivity.[17] One sees at work, on the one hand, attempts to establish a new civility amid the corrosive aspects of globalization. On the other hand, as older conceptions of class disappear, consumption options are threaded together as lifestyles in what Gerhard Schulze has called the experience society.[18]

For those who do not benefit so directly from the encounter of the global and the local, the cultural experience becomes not a newly discovered reflexivity or risk, but the experience of a culture of *survival.* Reflexivity is already part of life for the poor, the disadvantaged, and the migrant. The "double consciousness" of the dispossessed—of themselves and of how others view them—has long been part of their experience, chronicled already by W. E. B. DuBois in 1903.[19] Today, as Homi Bhabha has averred, "the truest eye may now belong to the migrant's double vision."[20] It is those who do not benefit who see both the promise and the profound contradictions that mark the encounter of the

---

[16]Featherstone, op. cit., 9.

[17]The work of Amitai Etzioni, Michael Walzer, Michael Sandmel, and Charles Taylor are being read extensively in the United States, the United Kingdom, and Germany. For an overview, see Daniel Bell, *Communitarianism and Its Critics* (Oxford: Oxford University Press, 1993).

[18]Gerhard Schulze, *Erlebnisgesellschaft: Kultursoziologie der Gegenwart* (Frankfurt: Campus Verlag, 1992), depicts some of the lifestyle options emerging.

[19]W. E. B. DuBois, *The Souls of Black Folk* (New York: Bantam, 1989).

[20]Bhabha, op. cit., 5.

global and the local. Culture becomes, Bhabha says later on, "... an uneven, incomplete production of meaning and value, often composed of incommensurable demands and practices, produced in the act of social survival."[21] In this experience of uneven, incomplete production of meaning, the process is experienced as oneiric, conflictual, and antagonistic.[22] Culture thus becomes a place of struggle in order to survive.

STRENGTHS OF GLOBALIZED CONCEPTS OF CULTURE

How would one assess the strengths and weaknesses of globalized concepts of culture? When one looks to the strengths, it is clear that these concepts try to reflect the experience of people living in a changing world today. Peace and harmony remain ideals, but they seem distant from day-to-day living. Life is experienced as fragmented, conflictual, and disoriented. Every aspect of culture, therefore, becomes an act of translation, that is, a piecing together, a transposition from one context to another, a struggle in the production of meaning.[23] And translations as cultural productions are ephemeral and fragile.

Second, globalized concepts of culture bring the problem of power more directly and centrally into the cultural equation. Sometimes all that is possible is resistance. Integrated concepts of culture, it may be recalled, did not deal with the problem of evil well. Globalized cultural concepts are better able to trace in their analysis of oppression the vagaries of power.

Third, integrated concepts of culture did not account well for social change, since change is seen as moving in the opposite direction from integration and homeostasis. Globalized concepts of culture, on the other hand, assume change as the normal state of affairs. But while change is expected and described, much still needs to be done to provide a theoretical account of it. The discussion of global theological flows and especially cultural logics is one such attempt. Dialectical accounts of change, perhaps the single most compelling theory, dominated discussions of change through much of the nineteenth century and well into the twentieth. But two things have altered the capacity of dialectics to account for change. First of all, there is a lack of *telos* to much of the change in a globalized world; it is simply change for change's sake, or change to create new markets of consumption. Without a *telos* there can be no move in dialectics from antithesis to synthesis. Second, our "*tiempos mixtos*" create what Robert Young has called

---

[21]Ibid., 172.
[22]Thus Young, op. cit., 7.
[23]Bhabha, op. cit., 226-29.

"incompatible, coexistent logics."[24] Given that situation, one cannot speak of the movement of history, since there are many movements at the same time, not all operating in linear fashion.

WEAKNESSES OF GLOBALIZED CONCEPTS OF CULTURE

Because of those incompatible, coexistent logics, globalized accounts of change remain theoretically weak as well. Globalization theory itself is an attempt to give an account of social processes, but it is still at a relatively early stage in its own development.

A second potential weakness lies with the theoretical assumptions behind globalized concepts of culture, at least in their postcolonial variety. By stressing the agonistic nature of culture, they succeed in providing a very credible phenomenology of contemporary experience. But it leaves open an anthropological question: are human beings and human societies fundamentally, even ontologically, violent? Many would appear to answer that question with a "yes," saying that inasmuch as globalizing processes run on the energy of capitalism, they are bound to be violent. Thus, for example, Robert J. C. Young: "the constant construction and reconstruction of cultures and cultural differences is [sic] fueled by an unending internal dissent in the imbalances of the capitalist economies that produce them."[25] But does not a critique of capitalist violence imply a peaceable alternative? Does not an ontology of peace need to ground the critique of violence? David Krieger's articulation of a "new universalism" has tried to do this.[26] If an ontology of peace has to undergird a critique of violence, how will this affect globalized concepts of culture, with their emphasis on asymmetry, conflict, and ephemerality? Major theoretical work has to be done here.

GLOBALIZED CONCEPTS OF CULTURE AND THEOLOGY

What is the significance of globalized concepts of culture for contextual theology? One might begin by noting that liberationist, feminist, and human rights theologies have already incorporated many aspects of these concepts of culture into their theologies. The problems of the exercise of power, the enduring issues of oppression, dislocation, and survival are recurrent themes in these theologies. While generally using modern rather than postmodern modes of analysis (although fem-

---

[24]Young, op. cit., 27.

[25]Ibid., 53.

[26]David Krieger, *The New Universalism: Foundations for a Global Theology* (Maryknoll, NY: Orbis Books, 1991).

inist work does include the postmodern), these global theological flows incorporate the issues explored in globalized concepts of culture even when using different methods.

What will a theology of culture look like using these concepts? What does culture mean for the cosmopolitan, for the migrant, for the refugee? Where are the moments of grace in the struggle for cultural translation? Where is God to be found in the midst of this? It seems to me that a theology of culture will have to focus especially on the moments of change rather than the moments of stasis. For it is in the experience of moving from one place to another, of cobbling together new identities out of the old ones, of negotiating multiple identities and logics that insight into where God is at work in a globalized culture will be found. It will be a study in surprise, in turning up the unexpected, in celebrating the small victories, for the experience of a globalized world lies in its peripheries, in the moments of risk and change, in the celebration of survival of yet another day.

Most especially, there will be a need to look at the asymmetries of culture rather than dwelling on the symmetries. The presence of asymmetry can signal a relationship of domination and oppression, but it can also portend novelty, the creation of the new. Symmetries tend to come to stasis, while asymmetries exhibit a restlessness that seeks new possibilities.

Two central Christian doctrines provide resources for exploring such a theology of culture, precisely through the endless creativity that flows from their asymmetries. The first is the doctrine of the Trinity, of God's triune existence. God's threeness and oneness, a subject of both puzzlement and wonder for Christians, is a source of asymmetry in relation to the world. The missions of the Second and Third Persons in the world, and God's reconciliation of the cosmos to the divine Being are themes that take on new significance in a globalized world. I believe that it is not coincidence that there has been an increased interest in the Trinity at the close of the twentieth century.[27] In an increasingly plural world, it is not surprising that the threeness of God should be receiving renewed attention.

The second doctrine that brings creativity in its asymmetry is the Paschal Mystery itself—the suffering, death, and resurrection of Jesus Christ. This doctrine has particular potential because it speaks of suffering, death, descent into the abyss of death, and being brought by the power of the resurrection not to the *status quo ante* (which would have been a symmetrical cycle), but to an utterly new place. It is that move to

---

[27]For an overview, see John Thompson, "Modern Trinitarian Perspectives," *Scottish Journal of Theology* 44 (1991): 349-65.

utter newness that reveals the asymmetry of the process. Christians have, I believe, a master narrative in this story for a time without master narratives; the story can help account for the suffering and death that stalk the world in a globalized era. It can accompany those who move through death into the bright light of the resurrection. The passion narrative itself brims with postcolonial ironies of betrayal, denial, mistaken identifications, and abandonment. And it ends in a great surprise.

An exploration of the asymmetrical resources of the Christian tradition, therefore, can contribute in new and creative ways to a theology of globalized culture.

In discussing the weaknesses of globalized concepts of culture, the question of violence and peace was raised, and how an alternative to an ontology of violence might be articulated. Can a nondominative form of universalism be found?

A theological proposal for such a universalism would be the theme of reconciliation, in the sense of God's reconciling the world. Reconciliation here is not a hasty peace that ignores the suffering of the world, nor is it an alternative to liberation and the struggle for justice. It can come about only through the end of suffering and the doing of justice. It represents God taking the world to a new place, transformed out of its suffering, but not forgetting the wounds of the past.[28] It is about overcoming the bifurcation of the world into those who benefit from the progress, equality, and inclusion that globalization systems promise, and the majority who do not. It is about addressing the urgent problem of what has been called the "two churches,"[29] a growing separation between the Church of the rich and the Church of the poor. Reconciliation portends to be a capacious enough theme both to recognize and struggle with the dividedness of the world, the fracturing of the world created by the compression of time and space, and the suffering of most of the world's population. It becomes a key aspect in understanding the new catholicity, a topic to which we will return in the final chapter.

CONCLUSION

This chapter has explored two sets of concepts of culture, both very much alive in the world today. Culture has become an increas-

---

[28]Robert J. Schreiter, *Reconciliation: Mission and Ministry in a Changing Social Order* (Maryknoll, NY: Orbis Books, 1992).

[29]The phrase comes from Michael L. Budde, *The Two Churches: Catholicism and Capitalism in the World-System* (Durham, NC: Duke University Press, 1992).

ingly important category for understanding the world and the construction of theologies. The first generation of contextual theologies used integrated concepts of culture to help assert local identity, and integrated concepts continue to be very useful in this regard. At the same time, the mixing of cultures today requires additional approaches. The fact of this mixing, and the new hybridities it is forming, probably explain why cultural analysis seems to be gaining ground over social analysis in much of the literature today. In a multipolar world, one cannot assume that the social structures are all the same, or that they are perceived in the same fashion. Social analysis assumes the ultimate rationality of society. Cultural approaches discern other rationalities in which the social structures analyzed by the Enlightenment are embedded. The concepts of culture flowing out of globalization theory help theorize the homogenizing influences coming into local cultures; postcolonial theory is an important resource for understanding how, culturally, local communities respond.

The role of agency, already noted as so important in intercultural hermeneutics' approach to intercultural encounter, clearly is much in evidence here. How cultures receive these homogenizing and often disruptive incursions depends on the quality and kind of their agency. While wealthy cultures can absorb the impact of globalization in postmodern options, the poor, who do not have these options, use a postcolonial approach to help create cultures of survival.

Globalized concepts of culture, as we have seen, go a considerable distance too in dealing with the social change that is part of globalization. While still not able to account for social change theoretically, their provisional responses at least create the possibility of survival. The grand dialectical philosophies of history of the nineteenth century no longer render a credible picture as they were once capable of doing, in that more short and medium term explanations are being sought.[30]

How does all of this converge on the formation of religious identities today? That is the topic of the next chapter.

---

[30]Featherstone, op. cit., 30.

4

Religious Identity:
Synthesis and Syncretism

INTRODUCTION

Syncretism continues to be an issue of great interest in the worldwide Church today, but there seems to be little theoretical advancement. Without some such advancement, it is unlikely that effective practical criteria will be found to ascertain the integrity and authenticity of Christian identity. The invocation of the word "syncretism" still summons up for many Christians images of compromising Christian faith or harmonizing faith with its environment at any cost. The *Synkretismusstreit* of the seventeenth century, in which Protestant divines tried to reconcile the doctrines that grew out of the Reformation splits, comes to mind for many Protestant Christians.[1] Or, syncretism evokes images of the decadence and dissolution of Mediterranean Religion in the Late Roman Empire.[2] And the pronouncements of theologians earlier in the twentieth century, warning against the dangers of indiscriminate mixing of religion (one thinks especially of the Dutch theologians Hendrik Kraemer and Willem Visser 't Hooft), still ring in many ears today.[3] Not to be vigilant against syncretism is to betray Christian faith. Certainly no Christian wants to undermine belief, but the endless disagreements among Christians about where the boundaries are bespeak a lack of clarity about the concept.

---

[1] For a discussion of this controversy and the most important figure within it, see Johannes Wallmann, "Calixt, Georg," *Theologische Realenzyklopädie*, vol. 7, 552-59.

[2] For a review of scholarship on syncretism in this period, see Carsten Colpe, "Syncretism," *Encyclopedia of Religion*, vol. 14, 214-27.

[3] Hendrik Kraemer, *De wortelen van het synkretisme* ('s Gravenhage: Het Boekencentrum, 1937); idem, *The Christian Message in a Non-Christian World* (London: published for the International Missionary Council by the Edinburgh

Syncretism is also a concept in the social sciences and in postcolonial writing. There it does not have the uniformly negative connotation it carries in Christian theology. In those settings syncretism refers to the formation of new identities out of cultural elements that are at hand, usually from more than one culture. A number of authors, including this one, have argued for this more positive understanding of syncretism—or at least a balance between the positive and the negative understanding. Focusing only on its negative connotation of compromising the integrity of Christian faith obscures the cultural dynamics by which an identity is formed. Rather than leading to any further insight, a pronouncement of syncretism in this negative sense simply stops conversation. And we have seen how important that conversation is to intercultural understanding. Other authors, while seeing the merit of this proposal, say the term is so heavily weighted with a theological history that it is beyond retrieval.[4]

In recent years two valuable collections have appeared on syncretism from a theological perspective, and a third one from a social science perspective.[5] These give hope that it is possible to make some advance in coming to terms with what is admittedly a crucial problem: Christian identity in the manifold cultures of today. And although one might wish for a word better than "syncretism" to describe the phenomena under study, Charles Stewart and Rosalind Shaw have raised a methodological point that bears reflection before discarding the term:

It also seems unnecessarily limiting to avoid a term which already exists to describe religious synthesis because of some of the connotations it has been given by (mostly) nineteenth-century scholars. On the contrary, embracing a term which has acquired—in some quarters—pejorative meanings can lead to a

---

House Press, 1938); W. A. Visser 't Hooft, *No Other Name: The Choice between Syncretism and Christian Universalism* (London: SCM Press, 1963).

[4]On the former position, see Leonardo Boff, *Church—Charism and Power: Liberation Theology and the Institutional Church* (New York: Crossroad, 1985); Robert Schreiter, "Defining Syncretism: An Interim Report," *International Bulletin of Missionary Research* 17 (1993): 50-53. On the latter, Peter Schineller, "Inculturation and Syncretism: What is the Issue?" Ibid., 16 (1992): 50-53.

[5]Jerald D. Gort, Hendrik M. Vroom, Rein Fernhout, and Anton Wessels (eds.), *Dialogue and Syncretism: An Interdisciplinary Approach* (Grand Rapids, MI: William Eerdmans, 1989); Hermann P. Siller (ed.), *Suchbewegungen: Synkretismus—Kulturelle Identität und kirchliches Bekenntnis* (Darmstadt: Wissenschaftliche Buchgesellschaft, 1991); Charles Stewart and Rosalind Shaw (eds.), *Syncretism/Antisyncretism: The Politics of Religious Synthesis* (New York: Routledge, 1994).

more challenging critique of the assumptions on which those meanings are based than can its mere avoidance.[6]

It is for that reason that I will use continue to use syncretism to describe the formation of religious identity, always with the understanding that at times the new identity under examination will be in accord with, and even enrich, the religious tradition; and that at other times, it will not be in accord, and so must be rejected. As we move toward examining what the criteria for proper theological identity might be and how they might be developed, it is worth remembering that there is a twofold process of identification and development here. On the one hand, we must attend to how religious identities are formed, especially at the present time. Those pathways are by no means uniform, and they frequently reflect the outcome of considerable struggle. To bypass reflecting on the formation of religious identity forecloses on dialogue, leaving the observer of the situation alone with preformed prejudices. Not to attend to how religious identities are formed is to assume that there is but one way, and it is the way of the observer of the phenomenon, and the observer fully comprehends it.

On the other hand, we must seek theological criteria for ascertaining the quality of the identity formed. This involves more than coming up with a list of possible criteria that are theological. The choice and the weighting of the criteria must also be theologically grounded. That is to say, a coherent theological rationale needs to be given for why these criteria should be operative.

This chapter moves through four steps. It begins by looking back at syncretism, with an eye toward unveiling assumptions that may be directing the syncretism discussion unbeknownst to its interlocutors. In a second step, the discussions of intercultural hermeneutics and conceptions of culture from the second and third chapters are taken up again to see what they might yield for the discussion of syncretism and identity. A third step explores the formation of religious identities, looking at a number of pathways: resistance, hybridity, and hierarchy. This third step concludes with some thoughts on the utility of the semiotics of culture for assessing religious identity formation. In a fourth step, the question of theological criteria will be taken up again.

This is all intended to be a continuation of the discussion of criteria for Christian identity, syncretism, and double belonging begun in *Constructing Local Theologies*.[7]

---

[6]Stewart and Shaw, op. cit., 2.

[7]Robert J. Schreiter, *Constructing Local Theologies* (Maryknoll, NY: Orbis Books, 1985), chapters 5 and 7.

LOOKING BACK AT SYNCRETISM

Reflecting on how Christians came to think of syncretism as they do may help reveal some of the assumptions and even prejudices that inadvertently shape the contemporary discussion. One might begin with reflections on the origins of Christianity itself.

From the perspective of religious development, one could say that Christianity began as a reform movement within the Judaism of its day. As a reform movement, it was one of many in the first century. It looked both backward to repristinate Jewish life, and looked forward, expecting to see its Lord coming again soon. As a reform movement rather than as an utterly new movement, it saw itself enacting a more faithful following of what God had revealed in the Torah. That faithful following entailed a vision of a purer path, from which unnecessary and even harmful accretions had been cut away.

Having begun as a reform movement has given Christianity a certain asymmetry, a certain restlessness. Time and again throughout history, groups within Christianity have taken up the call to reform once again: the desert dwellers of the fourth century, monastic founders, leaders of lay movements, the sixteenth-century reformers, and the Second Vatican Council. Its origins in reform give Christianity a vigilance that sometimes becomes an anxiety about the quality of faithfulness. To be sure, all Christians are concerned about faithfulness, but those who bear the memory of reform intimately as a part of their identity feel this most keenly. Any new development is potentially a deviation from the path, and any proposal that suggests an addition or amendment is potentially encumbering to pure faith.

People steeped in reform are conscious of boundaries and clear identity markers. Their sharp sense of identity is therefore at risk with any new proposal. This could be contrasted with other bodies in Christianity that emphasize comprehensiveness as a constituent feature of Christian faith.

The ethos of reform, of the *ecclesia semper reformanda*, pervades all of Christianity, but is more at play in some parts of Christianity than others. Compare it with Mahayana Buddhism where a great many pathways are tolerated because, in the end, any of them might just lead to Enlightenment. I think this basic assumption about reform and boundaries shapes how Christians approach discussion of syncretism. Calling attention to this assumption is not intended to urge Christians to go slack in their quest for deeper conversion and renewal. It is only to circumscribe it somewhat so that it becomes a partner in the inculturation discussion rather than a solo voice drowning out all the others.

A second consideration regarding syncretism has to do with the wide divergence of historical forms of Christianity in spite of common Scriptures and a (largely) common profession of faith. How does one account for the difference in form and ethos between East and West, between high liturgical and enthusiastic Pentecostal forms of Christianity? The cultural interaction in each locale is a decisive factor. James C. Russell's work on the Germanization of early medieval Christianity is one study of cultural interaction and religious identity formation.[8] He hypothesizes that "the worldview of the Indo-European, Greek, Roman, and Germanic religions was essentially folk-centered and 'world-accepting,' whereas the worldview of the Eastern mystery religions and early Christianity was essentially soteriological and eschatological, hence 'world-rejecting.'"[9] Russell claims that when Christianity spread through the Mediterranean it generally did not have to accommodate its world-rejecting worldview to its world-accepting environment because it was attractive to all those whose dissonant social status excluded them from full participation in the society of the Roman Empire anyhow. These were non-citizens, wealthy women, freed slaves, and immigrants from outside the Empire. Christianity promised these people full membership based on belief and behavior, not on ethnic identification or family status. That full membership included other-worldly salvation, clearly attractive to those who could not find it in this life. In the anomie of Late Roman imperial society, Christianity could propagate its message without significant alteration of its codes.

It was a different situation when Christianity moved into the Germanic north of Europe, where it adopted a policy of temporary accommodation to a highly vital society that enjoyed high levels of group solidarity (as compared to the anomie of the Mediterranean world). This temporary accommodation led to a transformation of Christianity itself, a transformation that from the tenth century onwards flowed back into Italy to become the cultural standard in Rome. And from Rome, it spread throughout the West.[10] The Christianity of the anomic urban society could not connect with the rural societies of the North, with their pastoral-agriculturalist and warrior culture. The difference is caught graphically in the retelling of the Gospel story of Jesus in that marvelous ninth-century poem, the *Heliand*. There the Galilean becomes a *drothin* or local warlord, caught up in the fate God has given him, who

---

[8] James C. Russell, *The Germanization of Early Medieval Christianity: A Sociohistorical Approach to Religious Transformation* (New York: Oxford University Press, 1994).

[9] Ibid., 4.

[10] Ibid., drawing especially on Josef Jungmann here.

tutors his twelve vassals in his ways.[11] The high level of group solidarity brought with it a clearer stratification of clergy and laity, marked by the growing distance between the altar and the people. The Christmas festival cycle came to rival the Easter cycle. More attention was given to objects (the cross, relics) and to Mary and the saints. Private votive masses were introduced. Praying with hands folded, the posture of a vassal before a lord, replaced the traditional *orans* posture.[12] In other words, a very recognizable pattern of folk religion was becoming part of European Christianity. Russell hypothesizes that the development of this kind of Christianity resulted from the cohesiveness of Germanic societies, from the failure to carry out doctrinal and ethical instruction after Baptism, and from the power of the Ottonian kings.

Taking just this single example, from a form of Christianity that shaped the West until the Reformation and lives on in popular religion exported to Latin America from the Iberian peninsula in the fifteenth century, one sees from a semiotic point of view what happens when the message of Christianity is transmitted via a different cultural code—in this case, a code of world-accepting. Given the changes that took place, is Christianity incompatible with such a cultural code? A reform-minded Christian might be tempted to say yes. The Christianity that emerged seems deviant from its Mediterranean ancestry. But if this position is held—that certain cultural codes are *a priori* incompatible with Christianity—would that not imply that the message of Christ cannot be communicated to all cultures? Or that certain cultures have to be destroyed in order to be saved? While it is possible to encounter cultural codes that appear to be incompatible (one thinks of the famous "peace child" story from Irian Jaya),[13] it is generally wise to be cautious about any condemnations of a premature nature—for both cultural and theological reasons.

As we shall see, it is the transmission of the Christian message via different cultural codes that is the nub of the syncretism problem. The

---

[11]For a study of this poem, see G. Ronald Murphy, *The Saxon Savior: The Germanic Transformation of the Gospel in the Ninth-Century Heliand* (Oxford: Oxford University Press, 1989).

[12]Russell, op. cit., 42-43.

[13]In Irian Jaya, evangelist Don Richardson and his wife were recounting the Passion narrative to the Asmat, who broke into cheers when Judas betrayed Jesus, because the ability to deceive is highly prized in Asmat culture. The Asmat eventually came to Christianity through the code of the "peace child," a practice whereby the child of a chief is given as hostage to a warring neighbor as a guarantee of peace. The Richardsons declared that Jesus was God's peace child. Don Richardson, *Peace Child* (Ventura, CA: Regal Books, 1975). One may, of course, question whether the peace child code and Christianity are compatible as well.

code, even more than the symbols that are taken from the material culture, is the source both of creativity and of frustration for Christian theologians, for it is the code that transforms the valence of the symbol. For example, the Maya had a cross (the four arms being of equal length) long before the advent of Christianity. Roughly speaking, it might be called a cosmic cross in that it brings together the directions, forces, and powers of the universe. It has been influential in the development of the colorfully painted Central American Christian crosses popular around the world today. Yet with the modern Mayan resurgence, the Mayan cross has become for some a countersymbol to Christianity—it has been reimbedded in a pre-Christian code.[14]

For understanding contemporary syncretism, then, even a brief look at the past reminds us of how much cultural interaction and symbolic transformation has always been taking place. From such a perspective, contemporary proposals that might seem daring become more modest in scope.

SYNCRETISM AND IDENTITY

"Fixity of identity is only sought in situations of instability and disruption, of conflict and change."[15] It is not surprising, then, that identity should be an issue in a time marked by the pressures of globalization, a time of migration, compression of space, and intense cultural interaction. In examining how religious identities are formed, it might be useful to reprise what has been said earlier about intercultural hermeneutics and concepts of culture. Bringing these discussions to bear specifically on the question of religious identity may help us see more clearly some of the dynamics involved in syncretism.

There are two things to be recalled from the intercultural hermeneutics discussion. First of all, the speaker and the hearer do not share exactly the same goals in the communication event. The speaker is concerned with getting a message to the hearer in such a manner that the hearer comes to understand the message in the same way as does the speaker. In other words, the speaker is concerned with the transmittal of the message in its integrity. The hearer, on the other hand, is pre-

---

[14]See Richard Wilson, *Maya Resurgence in Guatemala: Q'eqchi' Experiences* (Norman, OK: Oklahoma University Press, 1995); Kay B. Warren, "Transforming Memories and Histories: The Meanings of Ethnic Resurgence for Mayan Indians," in A. Stephan (ed.), *Americas: New Interpretive Essays* (New York: Oxford University Press, 1992).

[15]Robert J. C. Young, *Colonial Desire: Hybridity in Theory, Culture and Race* (London: Routledge, 1995), 4.

occupied with trying to make sense of the message—that is, relating it to other knowledge within the hearer's universe. Put another way, the hearer is trying to incorporate new knowledge. The speaker is on the alert for any alteration of the message that might compromise its integrity; the hearer is trying to make the message fit into an identity. The speaker is on the watch for syncretism; the hearer is struggling for synthesis.[16] Recall the evangelist in northern India: he wanted to convey the message that he wished to win the souls of the village for Christ. That was intelligible evangelistic rhetoric in the speaker's universe; perhaps the evangelist himself had undergone a sudden conversion in this manner. The hearers of this message in the village were trying to assimilate the message "win your souls for Christ" into their cognitive universe. "Winning souls" sounded like snatching souls, the activity of witches. And this stranger and his wife were known to have a cat, the familiar of witches. Therefore, they must be witches on the prowl for souls. The puzzling thing, of course, was why would the witch announce this rather than undertake his heinous task surreptitiously? And what was this Christ going to do with their souls?

This example illustrates a situation where syncretism is frequently invoked. Both sides are honest and willing in their communication. Both are working within the acceptable codes of their cultures. For the evangelist, winning souls for Christ is understood within a code of divine rescue from sin and perdition. For the villagers, winning souls is understood within a code of witchcraft, snatching souls for no good purpose. The speaker's message did in one sense get across, but its new encoding in the villagers' culture nearly reversed its meaning. Reencoding nearly always happens, since codes are the pathways along which messages circulate in a culture. Without those pathways, a message has no intelligibility. Winning souls was a message that circulated within a code of witchcraft, and once the evangelists' cat was sighted, the appropriateness of that code was only confirmed.

There is something here to be learned for the study of syncretism. The speaker perceives syncretism, which is for him a wrong religious identity. The hearers discover a witch, which confirms their religious identity. What this teaches us is that syncretism can never be discerned entirely from the side of the speaker. There is too great a risk of misreading the hearer's response. The expression of amazement on the faces of the villagers was likely misread by the evangelist as a response of wonder and awe. Speakers have to learn how messages get lodged in hearers' universes.

---

[16]See here John D'Arcy May, "Synkretismus oder Synthese? Eine antizipatorische Skizze des religiösen Wandels im Pazifik," in Siller, op. cit., 185-92.

One might object that the villagers simply got the message wrong. Recalling Stewart and Shaw's admonition to keep the term "syncretism" in order to uncover hidden assumptions, let us briefly examine the message "winning your souls for Christ." That kind of soteriological language assumes that there is a struggle over human souls, that they are not automatically on the side of Christ. There must be an alternative. The language of winning souls has to do with the battle between good and evil. So the villagers were really not very far off the mark. They recognized a code about the struggle between good and evil. And even if the evangelist were to get his message across using his code, that particular code would continue to evoke images of witchcraft, rather than replace it with the evangelist's own soteriological understandings.

The speaker alone, then, cannot decide finally that the message has been transmitted in its integrity. This brings us to the second thing to be recalled from the discussion of intercultural hermeneutics: meaning is established in social judgment, in the intense and repeated action between speaker and hearer. It only underscores the first point about the speaker not acting alone. For the churches it means that some tribunal, acting alone, will be incapable of establishing fidelity to or deviance from the Christian message in the intercultural communication event. Knowing the hearers' concern with synthesis, the speakers must interact intensively.

One of the things that emerges in this dialogue is the residual indeterminacy of the message itself. No matter how clear the speaker tries to be, indeterminacies in the message will be brought out as the cultural boundary is crossed. Every teacher and every preacher is familiar with this: in the interpersonal sphere, misunderstandings will arise based on indeterminacies in the message. Crossing cultural boundaries and reencoding the message brings out unnoticed aspects of the message even more strongly. Going back to the village example again: suppose the evangelist disavows any dealing with witches. But then the villagers hear stories from the Gospel about Jesus acting as an exorcist, or the accusations by Jesus' opponents that he casts out demons by the power of Beelzebub (Luke 11:14ff.). Every testing of a Christian utterance by speaker and hearer in the intercultural setting provides an opportunity, then, to reflect upon and deepen our understanding of the message itself, to acquaint ourselves with the indeterminacies that we had hitherto overlooked.

The discussion of the two kinds of culture concepts in chapter 3 offers some important insights for the study of syncretism as well. Integrated concepts of culture, because of their patterned nature, help us understand two things about syncretism and the formation of religious identity. First of all, they remind us that people do strive to live integrated lives: they try to incorporate new information into their cognitive universes in such a way as to live more full, human lives. The results of such attempts are seldom tidy or complete, since new information changes the cognitive universe as well. New information is never taken into a vacuum. It is always related to what is already known. Over time, that new information may come to have a prominent place in and transform a cognitive universe or worldview. But it always begins by relating to what is already known.

What this means is that what would be called a syncretistic idea in Christian theology is not formed by a process different from an authentically Christian one. Syncretic processes and synthetic processes are likely the same. From a semiotic perspective they have to do with the signs that are used to carry the messages (what other messages do they convey?) and the range of codes available as pathways for the circulation of messages. What new aspects of the message are called forth by a different code, both for the speaker and the hearer? It is the point of contact between the sign and the code, and what that does for the elaboration of a message, that needs greater scrutiny when there is suspicion of a misstatement on the part of the hearer.

A second insight to be derived from the reflections on integrated concepts of culture is that cultural purity is an impossible, even wrongheaded ideal. All cultures, even so-called traditional or small-scale ones, constantly adapt to their surroundings. Striving for cultural purity does not protect some pristine heritage. It is a cultural logic of reaction to an unstable situation. It is a strategy to declare certain ideas, performances, and artifacts as central to a culture's integrity and to be preserved at any cost. This has two implications for the study of syncretism and religious identity. First of all, new information is likely to change a culture. Put in terms of Christianity, the preaching of the Gospel cannot be done in such a way that the culture is left unchanged. This is so not only because of intercultural communication, but also because of the nature of the Gospel itself: it is a call to *metanoia*, to turning one's mind around. One can therefore also affirm the converse of this statement: if the culture does not change, the Gospel has not been preached!

Moreover, the Gospel never comes to a culture in pure form; it is already embedded in the less-than-pure culture of the speaker, the treasure carried in vessels of clay. Invocations of pure culture or even pure Gospel are not apposite, since here on earth at least, they do not exist. Introducing such ideas of purity into the syncretism discussion, then, does not really lead to the fidelity to the Gospel which we seek.

Globalized concepts of culture, drawing especially on postcolonial and globalization theory, propose cultures as a ground of contests in relations where we struggle with sameness and difference, comparability and incommensurability, cohesion and dispersion, collaboration and resistance. Diversity and difference are of great importance. The exercise of power in all its asymmetrical force never goes unnoticed. What do these concepts of culture contribute to a study of syncretism and religious identity? At least three things come to mind.

First, their descriptions of the world as one of struggle, multiple belongings, constant change, and only partial closure in the formation of identity come much closer to the experience of people everywhere today. Disruption rather than harmony is the day-to-day experience. Partial rather than total formation of self and community is the rule. Such descriptions allow the interlocutors in the intercultural situation to express their doubts, their puzzlements, and their misgivings about their understandings of faith rather than present them as imagined wholes. This can free the dialogue to be more authentic.[17]

Second, globalized concepts of culture foreground the role of power. Coercion and domination play a strong role in syncretism, both in forcing certain kinds of identity to appear, and in acts of resistance to such use of power. The asymmetries of power relationships must always be examined in situations involving new formations of religious identity. All too often it is the case that churches of wealthy nations align themselves against the emerging churches of poor nations, ready to deliver pronouncements of syncretism upon them. At the same time, those same wealthy churches are unwilling to see their own perversions of the Gospel message. One cannot, and must not, evade the question of power in probings of syncretism and religious identity.

Third, globalized concepts of culture give privilege of place to those asymmetries that spur creativity. In the previous chapter, the asymmetrical logic embedded in the central narrative of Christianity itself—the story of the passion, death, and resurrection of Jesus—was examined. In situations where people are struggling to articulate new Christian identities, one should attend to the asymmetries in these accounts, since they may be giving a new and deeper insight into the Gospel. The parables of

---

[17]Authenticity is also culture-specific, especially evident in cultures with strong codes of honor and shame, and of maintaining "face." What may and may not be said to strangers or those more powerful is understood differently from culture to culture. See William R. Cupach and T. Todd Imahori, "Identity Management Theory: Communication Competence in Intercultural Episodes and Relationships," in Richard L. Wiseman and Jolene Koester (eds.), *Intercultural Communication Competence* (London: Sage, 1993), 112-31; William B. Gudykunst, Stella Ting-Toomey, Bradford J. Hall, and Karen L. Schmit, "Language and Intergroup Communication," Molefe Asante and William B. Gudykunst (eds.), *Handbook of International and Intercultural Communication* (London: Sage, 1989), 145-62.

Jesus are deliberately asymmetrical, so as to draw the hearer into the story and make the hearer choose sides. Looking for such asymmetries reminds us that new Christian identities should be examined not just to be assured that they are not wrong, but also to see how they may be more profoundly right than we had imagined.

THE FORMATION OF RELIGIOUS IDENTITIES

Having explored aspects of religious identity illumined by intercultural hermeneutics and different concepts of culture, we can now turn to the third part of this chapter, which deals with the actual formation of religious identity. Again, this is intended to build upon what I have proposed earlier,[18] but reorders it in light of the discussion on culture above. Three types of formation of religious identity will be examined: formation through resistance, through hybridity, and from hierarchy. At the conclusion of the section, some further things will be said about the semiotics of culture.

RESISTANCE

Because power plays such a strong role in cultural encounter, and because that encounter is often intrusive, unequal, and violent, the reaction to the encounter is not infrequently resistance. Resistance can take the form of utter refusal to participate, or, if participation is forced, of withdrawal as soon as possible. One sees such resistance among the Pueblo peoples in response to their forced Christianization in the sixteenth century. An uprising effectively drove out the Spanish conquerors for nearly forty years. In some places churches were destroyed and *kivas* (the sacred assembly sites) were built on the same sites. Eventually the Spanish reconquered the area, but the Pueblo peoples to this day engage in a range of double belongings.[19] Often, however, such direct resistance is not possible. Then more selective forms of resistance are undertaken. The old religious ways go underground and are maintained in secret. Sometimes selective forms of resistance are possible in public. On the Santo Domingo Pueblo, for example, there are no Christian funerals, since all burials are done according to the "old ways." Christian clergy are not informed of deaths until all the rites have already taken

---

[18]Schreiter, *Constructing Local Theologies*, op. cit., chapter 7.

[19]For some of this history, see Ramon Gutiérrez, *When Jesus Came, the Corn Mothers Went Away: Marriage, Sexuality, and Power in New Mexico, 1500–1846* (Stanford: Stanford University Press, 1991).

place. In other instances Christian religious performance is followed, as in the veneration of the saints or the celebration of fiestas, but devotion is directed to other spirits as well. This is well documented in Afro-Brazilian and some Afro-Caribbean forms of Christianity.[20]

Among the native peoples of the Americas, and among those Africans transported there as slaves, a dense variety of forms of resistance and of survival can be found. These result in religious identities that continue to reshape themselves in new moments of conflict. It is not simply a return to the "old ways." The old ways are reinterpreted in light of the present. Richard Wilson has traced how the Q'eqchi' of Guatemala have moved from traditional Catholicism, to its leaders embracing liberation theology, to a reinterpretation of their Mayan heritage that sometimes entails the abandonment of Christianity altogether. Because many of the Q'eqchi' were displaced by the army, their relations with the mountain spirits (the *tzuultaq'as*), who are specific to a given mountain, were sundered. Those relations had to be recontextualized under new conditions in the Maya resurgence. As a result of this complex process, the *tzuultaq'as* continue to take on forms appropriate to their new contexts. In the nineteenth century they appeared to the Q'eqchi' dressed as German *finqueros* (plantation owners), and more recently they have appeared in military garb. Power is the common denominator. Wilson sums up the significance of this: "indeed identity should not be seen as a bounded Aristotelian concept but as an assortment of paradoxes that interact dynamically without ever being reconciled."[21]

HYBRIDITIES

A second set of identity formations might be called hybridities. Defined simply, a hybridity results from an erasure of a boundary between two (cultural or religious) entities and a redrawing of a new boundary. This has also been called "creolization," a hybrid of African slave and European New World language and culture. It is celebrated in contemporary Hispanic theology in the United States as *mestizaje*, the mixing of Native American and Spanish peoples.[22]

---

[20]On the latter, see Burton Sankeralli (ed.), *At the Crossroads: African Caribbean Religion and Christianity* (St. James, Trinidad and Tobago: Caribbean Council of Churches, 1995).

[21]Wilson, op. cit., 305.

[22]On creolization, see Ulrich Hannerz, "The World in Creolization," *Africa* 57 (1987): 546-59. For *mestizaje* see Virgil P. Elizondo, *The Future is Mestizo: Life Where Cultures Meet* (New York: Meyer-Stone, 1988).

In the nineteenth century, cultural and racial hybridity was much debated, with many holding that such mixing would lead to a diminishment of the strengths of the races, with the inferior race (i.e., African or Native American) overwhelming the superior one (i.e., the European).[23] This prompted advocacy for cultural and racial "purity," evidenced in the rise of miscegenation legislation, although a few remarked that even a superficial knowledge of European history showed that much mixing had already taken place, and that there was no "pure" white or European race. With the advance in knowledge of plant genetics by the end of the nineteenth century, hybrids could be seen as not just different, but potentially superior to unmixed varieties. But such knowledge had a hard time penetrating the prevailing racialist and cultural discourse.[24]

In my discussion of the varieties of syncretism and dual religious systems in *Constructing Local Theologies*, I described six types of mixing which now would be called hybridities. Regarding syncretistic phenomena:

(1) where Christianity and another tradition come together to form a new reality, with the other tradition providing the basic framework; (2) where Christianity provides the framework for the syncretistic system, but is reinterpreted and reshaped substantially, independent of any dialogue with established Christianity; (3) where selected elements of Christianity are incorporated into another system.

Regarding dual religious systems:

In the first set, Christianity and the other tradition are perceived as two distinct religious traditions, with both being practiced side by side. In the second set, Christianity is primary, with some selection of elements from a second tradition, which is nonetheless practiced separately from Christianity. In the third set, what constitutes religion in each of the systems becomes problematic as Christians try to remain faithful both to Christianity and to their national identity.[25]

While spoken of separately at that time, in terms of elements and religious systems, these six types can now be spoken of together in the

---

[23]As Young, op. cit., points out, much of the discourse of "race" in the nineteenth century is equivalent to the discourse on "culture" in the late twentieth century.

[24]Ibid.

[25]Schreiter, op. cit., 147-49.

contemporary discourse of hybridities. Most of the phenomena were looked at then in terms of the results of colonialism, where Christianity had initially been imposed on peoples or where its superiority and integrity had been stressed to the detriment of local religious forms. Those phenomena and those situations persist. But globalization, and the tensions between the global and the local, have become a seedbed for new varieties of hybridities, from New Age varieties that combine elements of Asian religions, Christianity, and native traditions of North America and pre-Christian Europe to African Independent Churches and the third generation of New Religions in Japan.

Hybridity is part of life in globalized cultures—either as an act of survival among the poor or as an act of choice in fashioning the self among the wealthy. From one perspective it can be seen as the latest stage of detraditionalization brought about by Enlightenment rationality, leading at best to an ever new "invention of tradition." But surveyed more carefully, there is at the same time a retraditionalization taking place in which elements of traditions are affirmed by their very inclusion in the scheme.[26] Traditions are often seen, especially by their guardians, as being more cohesive than they in fact might be. There are elements of indeterminacy in every tradition that make innovation possible.

Two final things need to be said regarding hybridities and religious identities. It was noted above that some people experience life as being in "tiempos mixtos," a combination of premodern, modern and postmodern existences. This experience can give rise to what Nestor Garcia Canclini has called "hybrid cultures," that provide strategies for moving between these different times.[27] As was noted in chapter 1, time was the primary metaphor of modernity, while space seems to be the metaphor of the postmodern. Because these three "times" are now coeval, hybrid cultures are constructions that allow pathways for moving between all three.

Hybrid cultures, these new constructions out of fragments of other cultures that serve as strategies for negotiating life in a globalized society, require religious identity construction commensurate with their situations. The more positive affirmation of popular religion in recent

---

[26]See Paul Heelas, Scott Lash and Paul Morris (eds.), *Detraditionalization: Critical Reflections on Authority and Identity* (Oxford: Basil Blackwell, 1996), which is as much about retraditionalization as it is about detraditionalization. See especially the essay of Timothy W. Luke, "Identity, Meaning and Globalization: Detraditionalization in Postmodern Space-time Compression," 109-33.

[27]Nestor Garcia Canclini, *Hybrid Cultures: Strategies for Entering and Leaving Modernity* (Minneapolis: University of Minnesota Press, 1995). First published in Mexico in 1989.

years as a legitimate way of experiencing God has been a step in that direction. The incorporation of indigenous religious traditions into Christian performance, especially in the Americas, has been another. One of the things that has become more and more apparent, at least from a cultural point of view, is that the reforms of the Second Vatican Council were addressed particularly to the challenges of modernity as experienced in secularized societies. Other cultural settings, while not ignored, were certainly not given the same kind of emphasis. This is not surprising, since introducing the language of culture into Church documents was still at an early stage. The ability to allow a number of religious forms to coexist, even when they cannot be completely reconciled, is providing for a hybrid religious identity appropriate to the times. The tensions are not resolved—centralization and inculturation within the Roman Catholic Church remain—but this should be viewed not as a problem to be solved, but as a source of a deeper life in Christ. It is an asymmetrical source for the development of new forms for carrying an ancient message.

The second thing to be said relates to the emerging discussion about "third cultures," that is, newly constructed cultures that mediate between two cultures.[28] The concept came first from programs for translation used by computers, where one language is translated into another language by passing through a third language which serves as a common basis for all translations. Perhaps what will be needed in a world of hybridities is such a third culture, which, while preserving difference in each of the cultures encountered, can serve as a kind of translation box through which communication can pass. This is an idea that still needs to be developed. Does, for example, the Vatican see itself as that kind of third culture for the Roman Catholic Church, mediating between local churches in terms of communication and practice? This is something to which we shall return in the final chapter.

Hybridity may be a fact of the globalized world, celebrating the diversity it creates. But all are not sure that this celebration of hybridity should be done uncritically. Robert J. C. Young, for instance, fears that hybridization will erase the discriminations of difference, leading us to take difference less seriously.[29] Ella Shohat reminds us that celebrating hybridity will legitimate the colonial violence that created it.[30] Both of these questions deserve further attention. If boundaries of difference now mark the globalized terrain as did boundaries of territory

---

[28]See, for example, Featherstone, *Undoing Modernity*, op. cit., 114. Homi Bhabha speaks of a "third space." See chap. 3, n. 11 above.

[29]Young, op. cit., 17.

[30]Ella Shohat, "Notes on the 'Post-Colonial,'" *Social Text* 31/32 (1992): 99-113.

at an earlier time, what legitimacy and durability should they be accorded? While it is all well and good to point out how communications technologies, such as the Internet, are constantly erasing boundaries, all of this presumes a relatively peaceful and equitable environment. What serves to guarantee and secure that environment? Second, boundaries also serve in the formation of identity. Those boundaries can be quite permeable, but they nonetheless help orient and situate people in the world. One can talk about the construction of the self in postmodernity, but one must also find ways of articulating life in community, since belonging is one of humanity's strongest needs.

That colonial hybridities were born of violence is something that must not be forgotten. Many contemporary hybridities into which people are thrown are of the same nature, where local social ecologies are disrupted by market forces, where members of different generations in a family of migrants are torn by loyalties to conflicting values. One must be careful, however, to distinguish critique of hybridities because they besmirch imagined purities from critique that addresses violence. Here once again the development of an ontology of peace may be central to engaging in an appropriate critique.

HIERARCHICAL FORMATIONS

The third formation of religious identity might be called hierarchical. By this is meant that church leadership or its intellectual elite try to move the cultural and religious mixing in a certain direction. At least three strategies are used to form religious identities in this way.[31] The first is a policy of tolerance, permitting a variety of possibilities to flourish within a circumscribed space. This can produce an easy or "soft" pluralism with an agreement that many things may flourish as long as they do not produce conflict. While superior to outright warfare, which is becoming more and more common again, it may also lead to a lack of commitment to any specific tradition.

A second strategy for identity formation is hierarchic encompassment, whereby church leadership moves to incorporate outside practices and ideas. The choice of the date December 25 to celebrate the Nativity of Christ was such an encompassment of the Roman Saturnalia, as was the introduction of evergreen trees into Christmas celebrations in northern Europe. Encompassment is a recontextualizing of signs and performances that may make identification with Christianity

---

[31]Following Rosalind Shaw and Charles Stewart, "Introduction: Problematizing Syncretism," in Stewart and Shaw, op. cit., 22.

easier for members of the culture, even as it brings change into Christianity as well.

Finally, new identities may be formed through legislation. Official church reforms by church or political leadership are intended to foster new identities. Such was the case in the sixteenth century Reformation in Europe. Official promotion of certain saints or special devotions have functioned to shape religious identities in Catholicism. For example, Our Lady of Fatima was clearly connected to anticommunism. With communism's demise, she is now directed especially against accommodation to Western-style consumerism. Legislation may work to make inculturation more possible (as in the vernacularization of the Roman Catholic liturgy after Vatican II). In those church bodies where legislation of this nature is possible, it can be a powerful force for expediting inculturation—or postponing it.

This review of different ways of forming religious identity is neither exhaustive nor taxative. Each represents a different way of approaching the issue of how identity takes shape. Knowing something of such processes is important for understanding their outcomes in the intercultural dialogue about syncretism and identity. If identities have been shaped as acts of resistance, dialogues with interlocutors perceived as oppressors will not go very far. The mixes in identities often need to be sorted out, but the mixing must first be accepted as a process by which genuine identity is formed. Hierarchical models can be used both to promote and to block inculturation. An ability to conceptualize how religious identities might be formed is an important part of entering the dialogue on syncretism and synthesis.

THE SEMIOTICS OF CULTURE AND RELIGIOUS IDENTITY

A final word here about the semiotics of culture as a means for understanding religious identity in its transformations. Culture was defined in chapter 2 as having *ideational* elements (worldview, values, rules about behavior), *performantial* elements (rituals and roles), and *material* elements (language, symbols, food, clothing, housing, and other artifacts). The semiotics of culture is concerned with the *messages* that carry identity and meaning in a culture, the *codes* that provide the pathways by which the messages circulate, and *signs* that relate the message (signified) to physical or mental elements within the culture (signifiers).

In a semiotics of religious identity as it crosses from one culture to another, the Christian message remains the same from culture to culture. That message is what Christians call the Gospel. But the message has an indeterminate character to it. That means that every detail and every aspect has not been made completely explicit. Furthermore, no message can be transmitted without using a code, and different codes will highlight different aspects of the message.

A culture embodies many codes, and a distinctive feature of cultural difference is the use of different codes. Thus, how to greet people and how to extend hospitality vary from culture to culture because codes for greeting and hospitality are different. In intercultural communication, learning how to read the different codes is key to understanding the message. It is therefore central also for being able to decide if the Christian message, differently encoded, has been able to maintain its integrity.

An example from Christian history might be useful here. Central to the Christian message is that "Christ died for us sinners" (Rom 5:8). What does that mean? The meaning of the message of Christ's death is communicated through different codes within the New Testament itself. Paul uses legal codes (justification, reconciliation), social codes (manumission from slavery), and ritual codes (atonement). A millennium later Anselm used the Germanic military code of honor to communicate this message as one of vicarious satisfaction. Anselm's proposal could be seen as an intercultural reading of Paul. Luther's doctrine of justification was another such reading of Paul, one that involved no mediation between the sinner and Christ. By placing the individual alone before God, without the agency of the Church, Luther was anticipating a central code of modernity that was just beginning to emerge in Western Europe—the autonomy of the individual in society. Today, African theologians and Pacific theologians are using initiatory codes to carry the message: Christ's death is his initiation into new life. His initiation allows him to be master of our initiation.[32]

The same message, therefore, is carried by different codes. Signs may come from either culture, although they will signify differently in each culture. The cross itself is an example of such a sign. Coming out of Mediterranean culture it was a sign of shame and humiliation. In northern Europe, it became amalgamated to the World Tree as a source of cosmic unity.[33] The cross could even become decorative (as in pro-

---

[32]For Africa, see Efoe Julien Penoukou, "Christology in the Village," and Anselme Sanon, "Jesus, Master of Initiation," in Robert Schreiter (ed.), *Faces of Jesus in Africa* (Maryknoll, NY: Orbis Books, 1991), 24-31 and 85-102, respectively. For the Pacific see John D'Arcy May, *Christus Initiator: Theologie im Pazifik,* Theologie Interkulturell, 4 (Dusseldorf: Patmos Verlag, 1990).

[33]This is well presented by Thomas H. Ohlgren, "The Pagan Iconography of Christian Ideas: Tree-lore in Anglo-Viking England," *Mediaevistik* 1 (1988): 145-73.

cessional and pectoral crosses). Signs therefore can oscillate between cultures and between codes within a single culture.

All of this is said to highlight the fact that in intercultural communication we look for the same message, circulating in different codes, utilizing a variety of signs.

THEOLOGICAL CRITERIA FOR CHRISTIAN IDENTITY

In order to establish authentic Christian identity in the intercultural setting, both communication and theological criteria must be used. In the previous three chapters intercultural communication elements and criteria have been discussed. These do not operate in a separate sphere from the theological; rather, they offer support for the theological elements by providing a context in which to understand them. In so doing, they may help us utilize the criteria more effectively.

Before moving to the criteria themselves, there are two formal considerations. First of all, there is an assumption that multiple criteria should be used, and that they should be used together, rather than making judgments on the basis of the use of a single one. This assumption derives not only from the complexity of Christian confession and performance itself, but also from the complexities of intercultural communication that have been discussed thus far. It would be hard to imagine how a single criterion could function effectively, especially in the intercultural context.

Second, each of the criteria will likely display a continuum of theological positions. This allows for the diversity of theological positions with the Christian ecumene, while still allowing some limit or control on the range of possibilities. For example, a criterion of "according to the Scriptures" might range from a position that understands this as what is explicitly taught in the Scriptures, to a position that what is proposed cannot contradict the Scriptures. The nature of a church body's ecclesiology will determine how important the opinion of other communities and church bodies may be in ascertaining the quality of the proposal.

Along with the two formal considerations, there is a material one as well. The churches need to develop theologies of culture. Many still rely on H. Richard Niebuhr's *Christ and Culture* or Paul Tillich's essays toward a theology of culture. These are very useful works. But they did not and could not take into account the intercultural situation that has developed so dramatically in the last half of the twentieth century. How might cultures be carriers of God's grace? How does God work in cultures before Christianity is even present, or continue to work outside the forms of the visible Church? A theological approach to culture that is explicit sets up guidelines that can be used in determining what may be embraced and what must be rejected, especially when it appears in signs and codes less familiar to traditional Christianity.

Five criteria were presented in *Constructing Local Theologies*.[34] Subsequent reflection has not led me to add to or subtract from them. But in light of what is known now about intercultural communication and the need for more explicit theological articulation, some nuancing of them can be done.

The first criterion, the cohesiveness of the Christian performance,[35] is concerned with how the proposal squares with Scripture and subsequent church tradition. Here the idea of continua that range from high to low understandings of Scripture and subsequent tradition, respectively, might be useful. All of these deal with how the message has been articulated in the past and what judgments have been made about those articulations. They deal, in other words, with both determinate and indeterminate aspects of the message. The message cannot be understood outside specific cultural encoding, yet no encoding ever exhausts its possibility. This would suggest that churches need not only a theory of Scripture and church tradition, but also one of development—what constitutes legitimate development in the articulation of faith?

The second and third criteria both look to the performance of the proposal, in the community at prayer and in its larger praxis. Again, continua may be useful to determine the relative importance of what each of these criteria might yield. The liturgical context is of consummate importance for Orthodox Christians, but does not hold the same power in Protestant free church traditions. Praxis will have high importance in communities with conjunctive epistemologies, where action and truth cannot be separated, but less power when thought is prized over action. Theologies of liturgy and action are necessary here.

The fourth and fifth criteria—accepting the judgment of other churches on the proposal, and a willingness to give judgment of the proposals of others—are tied, at the intercultural communication level, to the churches' communication across cultural boundaries. As was seen in chapter 2, meaning is established in the intercultural communication event in the social judgment of the hearer and speaker acting to-

---

[34]Schreiter, op. cit., 117-21.

[35]Performance as used in the five criteria follows Chomsky, who saw it as an enactment of a competence. See Schreiter, op. cit., 114. Performance as used in the definition of culture in this book refers to rites, roles, and behaviors.

gether. There must be intense and deep dialogue to establish the meaning and the truth of a Christian claim in the intercultural context. These criteria imply a theology of the Church and of the churches. They, too, admit of a continuum from high to low understandings of the church.

One sees in all the criteria, then, a need to develop a deeper theological base for understanding tradition, liturgy, action, and church. Rather than settling on handy formulae, a firm but flexible theology should help us appreciate the range of legitimate possibilities.

CONCLUSION

The meaning of the term "syncretism" will no doubt remain a contested issue, and for many will continue to bear a negative connotation. And it deserves to be contested, for it is about nothing less than the faithful transmittal of the Word that God has entrusted to us. At the same time, a better understanding of the complexity of intercultural communication, of the struggles for human and Christian cultural identity today, and an appreciation of the manifold, faithful ways in which Christianity has already manifested itself in history should ease our anxieties to some degree. They should make us more generous in listening to our brothers and sisters, more circumspect in how we speak, and always conscious of the treasures we bear in vessels of clay.

I have tried to argue here that, structurally, syncretism and synthesis are not different from each other. Both are attempts to form religious identity. A pronouncement of syncretism has been all too often a way of stopping conversation, of judging the outcome without attending to the process. In that sense, all change is syncretic and aims at being synthetic. Judgments about the outcome must be built on a genuine understanding of what is being said. The discussion of signs and codes was an attempt to provide a way into that understanding. Manuel Marzal has said that syncretism is the other face of inculturation.[36] The outcome will always bear surprises, because of a lack of full understanding of the culture, because of indeterminate aspects of the message itself, and because God continues to be at work among us.

---

[36]Manuel Marzal in Introduction to Marzal et al. (eds.), *El rostro indio de Dios* (Lima: Pontificia Universidad Catolica de Peru, 1991) (English translation, *The Indian Face of God in Latin America* [Maryknoll, NY: Orbis Books, 1996]).

5

The Future of Contextual Theology in Europe

INTRODUCTION

Contextual theologies first arose outside Europe and North America in reaction to the universalizing theologies of the West. The thought forms these universalizing theologies used, the methods employed, the questions raised, and the recurring preoccupations pursued were often perceived as alien—even alienating—to the countries then known as the Third World. Not only was so much of this theology foreign, it also hinted of a continued intellectual domination, even as political domination was being withdrawn at the end of the colonial period. The fledgling contextual theologies were frequently dismissed in Western academic settings as feeble and immature steps on the way to the development of a *real* theology, that is, a critical, rational theology that rose above the immediate situation to speak universally of God and God's action in history.

By the beginning of the 1990s the tone in the West was beginning to change. While it may still be too early to chart the change accurately (for it is by no means complete), some of the factors are emerging with greater clarity. First of all, the impressive developments in two forms of theology that worked far more contextually and deductively than standard academic theology—namely, liberation and feminist theologies—indicated that theological method might indeed be taking another direction. A greater use of the social sciences, themselves largely empirically based, pushed theology to remain more closely engaged with the concrete and the particular. Both liberation and feminist theologies were also oriented to action rather than remaining satisfied with intellectual clarification (although the latter was an important moment in their methods). This too set these theologies apart from a theology more centered in justifying its claims of knowledge vis-à-vis other cognitive claims in modernity. All in all, an alternative to how theology had been done in the universities began to thematize itself, even as some academic circles began to incorporate these methods and insights into their own research.

A second factor was the perceived distance between academic theology and an increasingly secularized society. As Christianity continued to lose ground in both the public and the private sphere, church leaders, pastors, and missiologists started looking for ways that theology might engage the secular context more effectively. The efforts to wed theology and context outside the North Atlantic region were scrutinized closely for clues as to what might be done in Europe itself. When various schemes were proposed for addressing the dechristianization of Europe—the New Evangelization in the Roman Catholic Church, the ecumenical Missiology in Western Culture project, the Gospel and Our Culture Project of the British Council of Churches—inculturation and contextualization were invoked as constitutive parts of those efforts.

A third factor was how the world as well as Western societies were undergoing change. Globalization in all its aspects—the collapse of the bipolar world and of socialism as an economic alternative, the dominance of neoliberal capitalism, the advances in communications technologies, and the migration of peoples—all are making the world a different place. When I was asked in 1992 to write a new foreword for the German edition of *Constructing Local Theologies*, indicating why that book would be of interest to a German-language readership, it was precisely to those changes that I pointed.[1] The interest in context in this instance had less to do with any perceived inadequacy of academic theology as it had usually been undertaken than with the speed with which changes were taking place, and the consequent destabilization of identities. Changes so momentous *had* to make a difference in how the world was viewed theologically. They could not be left unexamined.

In my estimation, it was principally through these three factors that the way was cleared for thinking about contextual theologies in Europe.[2] Over and above all of the other factors mentioned, at a time when the

---

[1] Robert Schreiter, *Abschied vom Gott der Europäer. Zur Entwicklung regionaler Theologien* (Salzburg: Anton Pustet, 1992), 13f.

[2] A case might be made for a fourth factor, the rise of the new practical theologies. These are a way of theologizing about practice, not merely an application of systematic theology to pastoral situations. See Don S. Browning, *A Fundamental*

European Union raises questions for European identity, it becomes important to take stock of just what are the prospects for contextual theologies in Europe. What aspects of European contexts should be engaged? What themes suggest themselves out of the Christian tradition for possible development? And what social issues need to be addressed?[3]

Europe is, of course, a vast and diverse place, as efforts at a European Union have made all too clear. A certain level of generalization is inevitable. There are some common features that might be treated, inasmuch as different parts of Europe are facing similar challenges. It is these common challenges that will serve as the focus of this chapter. Admittedly, even then this investigation will center more on Western Europe than on those countries formerly behind the Iron Curtain. Some of what will be said will, I hope, strike a responsive chord there, but in those countries history has given rise to a distinctive configuration of the problems of religion and society. And finally, this is being written by an outsider, albeit one who once lived in Europe and remains a frequent visitor. It is presented with the hope of stirring thinking in Europe about the future of contextual theology in that region of the world.

The investigation here is in four parts. The first three parts look at three salient factors at play in any future contextual theology in Europe. These factors are secularization, dechristianization, and the multicultural character of society. Each of these phenomena will be examined to uncover significant challenges for contextualization. Then, where possible, suggestions will be made regarding the contextualization process itself and what theological themes might be usefully taken up. The fourth and concluding part steps back to see what general conclusions might be drawn. It is hoped that in this way a framework for discussion of contextualization in Europe might be set up so as better to engage its possibilities.

SECULARIZATION

Secularization is a process that has been going on in Europe throughout the modern period. First understood as the appropriation of church property by non-ecclesiastical agents, usually the State, it has

---

Practical Theology (Minneapolis: Augsburg Fortress, 1992); Dietrich Rössler, Grundriss der praktischen Theologie (Berlin: Walter de Gruyter, 1994).

[3]Some efforts at contextual theology have been undertaken. See, for example, John Reader, Local Theology: Church and Community in Dialogue (London: SPCK, 1994). The attempts to develop a liberation theology in or for Europe seem to me to miss the mark.

come to be understood as the disengagement of religious rule and influence in modern society, on both an institutional and a personal level. In
the 1960s, a great deal of attention was given to religion's place in secularization, and attempts were made to celebrate humankind's "coming
of age" (to echo Dietrich Bonhoeffer[4]), with its celebration of human
autonomy. All of this was framed in the work of Max Weber, who saw a
continuing diminishment of religion under the forces of modernity.

Changes that have come about in understanding secularization are
leading sociologists to amend their theories of secularization. These
changes are necessary as changed circumstances in secularized societies pose new challenges to aspects of theory. There are four such
changes that have had an impact on the construction of contextual theologies in Europe.

The first is that religion has not disappeared. In an earlier stage of
modernity, predictions about the eventual disappearance of religion
were quite optimistic. To be sure, there has been a decline in the presence of religion in Europe, or at least of institutional religion. Church
attendance, as well as church baptisms, weddings, and funerals continue to dwindle. Yet there are two areas in which religion persists.

The first may be found in the cultural logics of antiglobalism, especially fundamentalism. It may be recalled that cultural logics are responses to the encroachments of globalization, affecting the local in
different ways. Fundamentalism, a slippery concept, is understood here
as choosing certain (usually patently antimodern) elements of a tradition and raising them up as the ultimate criteria of orthodoxy. Not all
conservative or even reactionary movements are necessarily fundamentalistic. Nearly all such movements continue to participate in modernity
in certain ways.[5] But they all share a revulsion for some, and sometimes all, elements of modernity.

The speed and pressure of globalization are such that it will likely
continue to provoke new fundamentalisms. The destabilizing of identities will be met with resistance and hoped-for reversion to more stable
times. A problem for contextualization is that religion as a whole now
comes to be identified in the eyes of its despisers with these fundamentalisms. They represent the passion that religion can call forth, even as
they skew the intellectual and symbolic universe from which religion
derives. Fundamentalism, as an act of resistance, can become a powerful local theology that no form of persuasion can change. Some forms

[4]See his *Letters and Papers from Prison* (New York: Macmillan, 1953).
[5]A good guide to the fundamentalist phenomenon is Bruce Lawrence, *Defenders of God: The Fundamentalist Revolt Against the Modern Age* (San Francisco:
Harper and Row, 1989).

of Pentecostalism function in a fundamentalistic way, and provide the poor an antimodern haven in a world that forces change on them without any of the benefits that change might bring.

A contextual theology in a European setting should not strive for a fundamentalistic goal, of course. But it must understand what drives people into fundamentalism. This is especially important for those segments of the population in Europe that have no other recourse in shaping their identities.

A second area in which religion is not disappearing is in the diffuse religiosity that continues to mark secularized societies. Because of its eclectic and usually privatized character, this religiosity is often not institutionalized. It appears to be the ultimate reduction of religion to consumption. At this time it is estimated that nearly one-fourth of Northern Europeans believe in reincarnation. In the United States in recent years there has been intense interest in and discussion of angels. All of these elements together—bits of Asian religion, interest in Western esotericism or pre-Christian European religion—are commonly known as New Age religion. New Age represents a fund of religious possibilities out of which new identities may be constructed. They are the grist for the syncretic mill which creates new hybrid identities.

This diffuse religiosity is usually dismissed as being beneath the dignity of consideration by religious leaders and elites. But a careful study of practices, rather than an exclusive focus on ideas, will yield up emerging patterns of religion. They are not likely to replace historical religions, but may come to be accommodated along any of the pathways discussed in the last chapter in the section on the formation of religious identities.

The second shift affecting an understanding of secularization is the tempering of optimism about human autonomy. The sometimes heady writing about the blossoming of human autonomy, the forward-looking visions of the theologies of hope, and the assessments that humanity had "come of age"—all hallmarks of the 1960s—began to be toned down, and at times even muted, in the 1970s by the OPEC embargo, the Report of the Club of Rome, and the growing awareness of potential ecological catastrophe. By the 1980s, rather than proclaiming a humanity come of age, postmodernists were predicting the death of the subject. The latter part of the 1990s is likely to witness an upsurge of apocalypticism and millennialism as the year 2000 approaches.

The instabilities that accompany globalization and the perils of the global economy make for a more circumspect view of human autonomy. Human autonomy is after all the goal of the secularization process, but it continues to be thwarted along the way. Since the struggle with bondage and the quest for liberation is so much at the heart of the Christian message, a contextual theology in Europe today must pick up on the changes in fortunes that have prompted this rethinking. What does the Christian doctrine of the atonement mean under these circumstances? How does one experience liberation in these days? The next chapter will look at future directions that liberation theology might take, but for now it is enough to focus upon the nexus of bondage and liberation as it has been playing itself out in recent history.

The third shift in the understanding of secularization is closely related to the second one and figured also in the earlier discussion of globalization itself, namely, the increase of risk in a globalized society. The heightened risk from the processes of short-term, swiftly moving global capitalism and ecological degradation have already been mentioned. Pharmaceutical risks can be added to these. Even as nuclear risk has subsided, risks of smaller, intense wars and the "coming anarchy"[6] of mass urbanization have arisen to create other threats. What happens in the wealthy centers is that even as they move to eliminate some risks (e.g., by establishing gated communities), they may be inventing new ones (such as toxic waste) or find that they have no control over others (e.g., they cannot isolate themselves from certain ecological disasters).

The management of contingency[7] is already a well-known concept in the sociology of religion. Just as a meditation on recent turns of events that question human autonomy will prove useful for emergent contextual theologies in Europe, so too will a reflection on risk and contingency. The increase in numbers of security guards and the outlay for security measures (in the United States there are now more private security guards than members of the public police forces) indicate the level of anxiety. The heightened sense of risk and contingency creates more space for religion as well. Religion should not be seen as a stopgap for plugging the holes in a porous sense of security. But it must also be remembered that risk and contingency are among the deepest themes in Christianity. Conversion, faith, and covenant all evoke risk. Our understanding of history and its fulfillment, our awareness of the asymmetries in the central Christian narrative of the suffering, death, and resurrection of Jesus cannot but remind us of the long reflection on contingency in our tradition.

The fourth and final consideration concerning the shifts in secularization is the release of alternate rationalities into society. Ulrich Beck refers to this as a "secondary scientization" of knowledge. In the primary scientization of knowledge, the emergent physical sciences worked to

---

[6] See Robert D. Kaplan, "The Coming Anarchy," *The Atlantic Monthly* (February, 1994): 44-76.
[7] The concept of Kontingenzbewältigung was first developed by Niklas Luhmann.

convince Europe that only their—scientific—knowledge constituted the true knowledge that provided access to reality as it is. But science and scientific method, despite their phenomenal successes, still sometimes fail or contradict themselves. (Think, for example, of the contradictory results of research showing what is or is not healthy nutrition or what does or does not cause cancer.) Moreover, science has failed to solve some problems, again particularly related to health. By redoubling its efforts to convince the public that it is the only rationality, it unintentionally gives legitimation to other, competing rationalities.[8]

Such legitimation in turn allows still other rationalities to flourish, even though they may not stand up under much scrutiny. Contemporary belief in reincarnation in Europe is an example of such an alternate rationality. A contextual theology in Europe today needs to trace the rationalities, in all their hybrid forms, as they crisscross the continent. The rationalities often intermingle along the way. Take, for example, the renewed interest in the pilgrimage path to Santiago de Compostela, which attracts tens of thousands of people each year, especially young people. The medieval pilgrim road now becomes a hybridity of Christian asceticism, esotericism, history, tourism, and pre-Christian religion.[9] A semiotic disentanglement of rationalities is a first step toward discerning the directions in which a new local theology might go, especially as it meets the quest for identity, the management of risk, and the encounter with contingency.

Secularization, then, is offering a number of new openings for the place of religion in society today. Contextual theology is not determined by what secularization may or may not offer to it; were that the case it would never be able to exhibit its prophetic edge. But a contextual theology in Europe has no choice but to take secularization into account. What is emerging in recent years is that secularization is not a uniform force, moving on a clearly chartable trajectory. It too is subject to changing forces in the environment. Contextual theology needs to be reminded of this, lest it acquiesce too readily to secularization's claims.

DECHRISTIANIZATION: THE POST-CHRISTIAN SOCIETY

Since the "loss" of the working classes to the Church in the nineteenth century, there has been talk about the dechristianization of Eu-

---

[8]Ulrich Beck, *The Risk Society: Towards a New Modernity* (London: Sage, 1992), 155-82.

[9]An example of such a weaving together is Juan G. Atienza, *En Busca de Gaia* (Barcelona: Robin Book, 1993).

rope. In the latter half of the twentieth century talk of a post-Christian society emerged. Beyond acknowledging a steadily diminishing influence of the Church as an institution, it is not always clear just precisely what is meant. The various projects and schemes proposed since the 1980s to rechristianize Europe—the New Evangelization of the Roman Catholic Church, the ecumenical Missiology in Western Culture Project, or the British Council of Churches' Gospel and Our Culture Project—all work toward a restoration of Christian faith to the populace of Europe. Before examining the implications of this for a European contextual theology, two clarifications need to be made.

First of all, dechristianization is not entirely coextensive with secularization. To be sure, the secularization process is usually held responsible for the drift away from Christianity. But if any of the aforementioned projects is successful in bringing Christianity back to Europe, it will not be to the Europe of Christendom. The migration of peoples, to be discussed further in the next section, has forever changed that. On the continent there is now a large Muslim presence that has resulted both from invitations to come and work extended in the middle of the twentieth century and from migrations and refugee flight that took place in the latter decades. In Britain there are Muslim and Hindu populations, as well as a smaller Buddhist population, all coming from throughout the Commonwealth. A new Europe will be an interreligious Europe.[10]

Second, a post-Christian Europe does not mean a non-Christian Europe. As Karl-Josef Rivinius has pointed out, much of the cultural heritage of Europe is unintelligible without an understanding of Christianity. Even the most secular of Europeans has imbibed and appropriated a great deal of Christianity in the values, understandings of justice, and other principles that are of the web and woof of Europe today. Even some values once thought antithetical to Christianity (such as democracy and human rights) are now seen to be legitimate developments of the Christian tradition.[11] One could argue, as Rivinius does, that any contextual theology that might be developed must lift up this Christian heritage and bring it to the attention of secular Europe. Following such a strategy, this would be the way to rebuild Christianity in Europe, by retrieving the foundation and then building upon it anew.

---

[10]See the explorations of the implications of this for Christians in Henk Vroom, *Religie als ziel van cultuur: Religieus pluralisme als uitdaging* (Zoetermeer: Meinema, 1996).

[11]Karl-Josef Rivinius, "Neuevangelisierung in Europa von 'nachchristlichen' Gesellschaften unter multikulturellen Bedingungen," *Theologie der Gegenwart* 36 (1993): 252-71.

A strategy like this may provide a partial answer to the New Evangelization, but there are some other paths to be explored in light of the larger considerations that frame this book. The globalization process destabilizes identities and creates the need to construct new ones. It does this with a speed and a complexity that make any institutional guidance difficult. Moreover, the individualism fostered by the modernity process and the cult of consumption leads to institutional distrust. If a society provides enough wealth to individuals to allow for a broad range of consumer choices, the illusion can be fostered that institutions are not necessary.[12] Emblematic of this belief in a life without mediating institutions is the Internet, which nobody owns and nobody controls, but upon which anyone with a personal computer and a modem can surf.

However, societies need mediating institutions between the individual or family and the nation. Religion, dethroned from the higher parts of the hierarchy, has tried to take that role in modern society and to some measure has succeeded when it has been a voluntary association. This is evident in the free churches, parachurch movements such as Campus Crusade for Christ, voluntary communities such as the Thomas-Community in Helsinki or the San Egidio community in Rome, and in the new religious movements.

Taking a cue from these institutions and associations that serve a mediating role, it would seem to be the task of the Christian Church today to establish credible communities, places that engage the power of ritual[13] and create group solidarity. In environments like these, practices can be cultivated and spiritualities evolved that could initiate people gradually and ever more deeply into the Christian mysteries. These communities would have to navigate between the antiglobal cultural logics that pull people toward fundamentalism on the one hand, and the primitivist cultural logics that urge people back to an imagined past on the other. These paths begin with religion as a way of life and move from there into the view of life, something which seems to fit the pattern of religious exploration: if the group is credible and inviting then the ideas may get a hearing.

In view of dechristianization, what elements would be highlighted in a contextual theology in Europe? Certainly a theological anthropology, stressing human creation in the image and likeness of God and the

---

[12]See the examination and critique of this position in Robert N. Bellah et al., *The Good Society* (New York: Harper, 1991).

[13]This is explored in Karl Gabriel, "Ritualisierung in säkularer Gesellschaft. Anknüpfungspunkte für Prozesse der Inkulturation," *Stimmen der Zeit* 212 (1994): 3-13.

worth and dignity of each person would be essential. In communities struggling with oppression, the emphasis on how human rights are now included in Christian anthropology could be made. When people are struggling with human identity and with human survival, anthropological issues are at stake.

It was mentioned above that the asymmetry of the basic Christian story, of the suffering, death, and resurrection of Christ, brings a special significance to identities in a globalized society. The basic story at the center of Christianity is not about symmetries, but about mistaken identities, betrayal, reversal, and a resurrection that is not restoration but that takes the crucified Jesus to a new place. In the asymmetries eddying out of the globalization process, with its maldistributions of power and profit, with its uprootedness, double visions, and multiple belongings, with its tentative hybridities—does not the paschal mystery take on new meaning, illumining these realities in a special way? Contextual theologies need to be able to read the Christian tradition in this way in order to connect it with the experience of many people today.

A MULTICULTURAL REALITY

Secularization and dechristianization are in themselves formidable challenges to an adequate contextualization. Added to this for contemporary Europe is the fact that many cultures are jostling each other within limited space and competing for limited resources. Although Europe is less culturally diverse than Australia or North America, it has a much longer history of ethnic territoriality than either of those continents. Multiculturality has come upon Europe in a much shorter period and at a time of uncertain identity in general. The diversity is to some degree of Europe's own making as one-time colonials settle in the imperial mother country; some people have also been invited in as cheap and additional labor, with the mistaken expectation that they will one day go back to their place of origin. In other cases, groups have been minorities within current national borders for a long time— the Basques in Spain, the Bretons in France. Sometimes people have migrated on their own, either from within Europe (Paris is now the second largest Portuguese city in the world) or from without, looking for work. One of the reflexive consequences of globalization is that now the peripheral peoples in the world economy can migrate to the center, and so the poor come to wealthy nations. Some immigrants are refugees from violence.

People from other ethnic groups do not just come and settle, they change the self-understanding of those longer settled there. Xenophobia sometimes breaks out, the relationship between ethnicity and nationality is challenged (what does it mean to be German or French?), and the host culture is changed, subtly or not so subtly, despite any resistance the host country may mount. As cultures jostle against one another and even come into conflict with one another, how does one begin to form a local theology? Whose culture forms the basis?

As was seen in chapter 3, concepts of culture as integrated wholes do not work in these settings. As cultures compete, culture itself becomes a conflictual element. Culture becomes the force-field in which new identities are enacted. In the cultural logics responding to this dimension of globalization, ethnification takes place. Those cultural groups arriving in a new place experience their cultural identity differently from what it had been at home. Here they are a minority, where they may have been a comfortable majority at home. Here they may experience racism for the first time. They are always feeling the powers in conflict over how identity is to be formed. Similarly, the host country takes on a new awareness of its own identity as a culture. These changes in cultural awareness and self-understanding are part of the process of ethnification—the process of coming to understand one's own identity in terms of that of others, acknowledging the boundary of difference. The powerful host country can deny this and require either separation or assimilation on the host country's terms. But such demands are never wholly successful. Often in this process ethnogenesis takes place, i.e., a group coalesces around an identity that they had not had before, as when two groups who were in conflict at home come together under the common threat of hostility from the host country.

Contextual theologies were born in the ethnification process—either in the assertion of a local culture's distinctiveness against Western incursion, or in the affirmation of a local culture as a worthy bearer of the Good News of Jesus Christ. The multicultural reality of contemporary Europe calls forth a new challenge to contextual theology. How can a contextual theology negotiate diverse, even competing and conflicting cultural demands?

It seems to me that one must begin with a clear understanding of what a multicultural society is and what it might look like. To develop a full-scale model of a multicultural society goes beyond the scope of the discussion here; but a sketch can be given that would indicate the directions and the tasks of a contextual theology in such a society.

A successful multicultural society must begin by assuring that all groups have access to the means for a human life (housing, employment, education, medical care) and are protected from physical violence. While this may seem an unattainable goal, to the extent that it is not achieved any attempt at a multicultural society will remain unstable.

There are three stages in the development of a multicultural society. The first is recognition of diversity. Recognition is understood here not simply as a notional acknowledgment, but as an act of acknowledging awareness and legitimacy. It is recognition in the sense that the term has been developed by Axel Honneth, Charles Taylor, and others.[14] Without recognition there is invisibility, which demeans and dismisses those who are different. The recognition of diversity is more than acknowledgment that there are a variety of different peoples present, for that can lead merely to a generalization of otherness. Recognition of diversity requires recognition of each group, even though those recognizing may not know much about them.

From the point of view of contextual theology, the key issue is the identity of each group. Here again, a theological anthropology that stresses each being made in the image and likeness of God forms a good point of departure, particularly when posed as the question: what is it about us that makes us the image of God? The image of the addressees of the First Letter of Peter, the "exiles of the Dispersion" (1:1) may provide a frame, much as the early Church brought together in cities those of marginal and dissonant social status.

The second stage toward a multicultural society is respect for difference. Respect goes beyond acknowledgment of the otherness of diversity; it explores the nature of the difference and the consequences for living together. It is aware that not all differences can be adjudicated into sameness. Respect for difference moves beyond recognition. It requires struggling with the meaning of difference.

As a theological move, respect for difference involves a struggle against those forces in society that, using the signifier of race or other means of demarcation, make difference a warrant for discrimination and oppression. Theologically, respect for difference involves a praxis of struggle against sin and evil. Here, a theological reflection on racism can serve as a helpful resource.

The third stage toward a multicultural society is a forum of cooperation and communication. Those who have been in the struggle for justice together can see better what one group may contribute to the other and to the common good. Avenues of cooperation can be laid out. The forum aims to create a communicative society rather than another cutthroat marketplace.

Theologically, the vision of reconciliation in Ephesians 2 could be used here: the creation of a space where we are "strangers and aliens

---

[14]Axel Honneth, *The Struggle for Recognition: The Moral Grammar of Social Conflicts* (Cambridge: Polity, 1995); Charles Taylor, *Multiculturalism and "The Politics of Recognition"* (Princeton: Princeton University Press, 1992).

no longer" (2:19). Again, this stage requires more than the good will of the participants; it needs also economic and social justice. While aware that this stage will not be fully achieved in society, the utopian vision of Pentecost, of each hearing the Good News, but in their own tongue (i.e., without having to deny their identity), keeps the hope alive.

Europe has been struggling with the issues of secularization and dechristianization for quite some time. The multicultural society is still something relatively new. In an essay on the Turkish presence in Western Europe, British cultural geographer Kevin Robbins has proposed that Europe will come to terms with a new multicultural identity only if it undergoes a profound transformation based on the awareness of the violence that it has done to other cultures and to the region.

> One cannot be optimistic. There are no solid grounds for be-
> lieving that Europe might re-commit itself to the historical
> process. Is it actually capable of transforming its perceptions
> of the 'non-Europe' that surrounds it? In order to do so it
> would need to rid itself of its myths of the others, and to allow
> that they are real, diverse and complex peoples. It would have
> to dissipate these myths in order to understand the part it has
> played in the disruption and destruction of their cultures and in
> the turmoil and violence that have afflicted the region. That
> would mean accepting its responsibilities in the events of past
> history.[15]

CONCLUSION

What then may be sought for in the future of contextual theologies in Europe? Like contextual theologies anywhere, they must be developed in accord with the local contexts, engaging the culture effectively and appropriately, yet critically. Effectiveness entails a genuine engagement and not just a superficial encounter. Appropriateness requires engagement in such a way that the culture's codes are respected. Critical engagement means that critique is part of the process, within parameters of effectiveness and appropriateness.

Salient cultural characteristics for contextual theology in contemporary Europe were identified within the frame of the effects of globalization, especially secularization, dechristianization, and the reality of a

---

[15]Kevin Robbins, "Interrupting Identities: Turkey/Europe," in Stuart Hall and Paul du Gay (eds.), *Questions of Cultural Identity* (London: Sage, 1996), 81f.

multicultural society. Each of these requires specific theological moves. Furthermore, four formal principles need to be kept in mind.

First of all, theology must be in forms intelligible to its communities, but also in forms commensurate with how meaning is being shaped in contemporary society. Thus, the impact of communications technologies needs to be taken into consideration.[16] Likewise, the meaning formation process in ethnification must be followed out.

Second, a key task of any contextual theology is the negotiation of identity in a globalized world. That entails knowing something of the globalization process and its consequences for identity formation. It is on that basis that a critique of globalization can then be mounted. A contextual theology will thus stand between tradition and modernity.[17]

Third, given the globalized context, a contextual theology will have to be able to utilize paradox and contradiction in an effective way, inasmuch as globalization is shot through with paradox (global-local relations) and contradiction (promising one thing, delivering another). Both of these are necessary to communicate the effects of globalization in a contextual theology.

Fourth, contextual theologies are grounded in communities and movements. Within those communities and movements there must be developed a theological base out of which local theologies can grow. That base includes (1) an anthropology that meets the challenges of contingency; (2) a spirituality, grounded in the paschal mystery, that negotiates risk; and (3) a utopian horizon for cultural inclusion and transformation.

---

[16]See especially in this regard the proposal of Antonie Wessels, *Europe, Was It Ever Really Christian? The Interaction of Gospel and Culture* (London: SCM Press, 1994).

[17]See Karl Gabriel, *Christentum zwischen Tradition und Postmoderne* (Freiburg: Herder Verlag, 1992).

6

Liberation Theology between Resistance and Reconstruction

CHANGES IN EVENTS, CHANGES IN THEOLOGY

A major focus of this book has been the changes that have taken place in the world, and how these in turn call for changes in theology. For any theology that pays serious attention to its context, this should be a foregone conclusion. Whether one begins with the context and moves to theology, or one begins with theology and moves to the context, changes in context have to be taken into account by theology.

The emergence of globalization has been one such change that we are trying to follow here. It will be remembered that one of the key moments in the consolidation of the forces of globalization was the collapse of socialism in Eastern Europe. This ended, both economically and politically, an important bipolarity in the world that grounded in turn a form of bipolar thinking about the world. Having become so accustomed to bipolar thinking, how does one shift to another kind? How does one deal with a plurality of centers, rather than two opposing poles? Bipolar views of reality could privilege dialectical thinking, but what happens when we are confronted with multiple discourses that may not even be commensurable? It is no wonder that, under such circumstances, discourses of postmodernity have come to the fore. They seem to account for, in general, this sometimes perplexing multiplicity of discourses (although not actually relating them one to another).

In this presentation, I wish to look at a major form of theological discourse in order to investigate how it is changing and needs to change because of the challenge of a change in context. That form is the theology of liberation. It is a major form because it represents what is likely the largest and most pervasive global theological flow, that is, an interlocking set of mutually intelligible discourses that together form an antisystemic global movement addressing poverty and political oppression in the world. It is made up of discourses that are anchored in specific contexts and address issues of poverty and political oppression in those contexts. Yet the discourses bear enough commonality to be understood in other settings, and the interaction among them creates not only mutual understanding, but also bonds of solidarity. The issues for a theology of liberation are not the same as those that stimulated a Black theology of liberation in South Africa; nor are either of these the same as those which prompt dalit theology in India. Yet they all represent, in different ways, what Gustavo Gutiérrez has called "the irruption of the poor." They form together an antisystemic global movement, unmasking the lie of promises of progress, equality, and inclusion in the economic global system.

It is important, then, to look at liberation theologies, not only because of their sheer pervasiveness, although that in itself would be sufficient warrant to do so. They are important because they give voice to the aspirations of what may be the majority of Christians in the world, struggling with poverty and oppression. How can such voices go unheeded? And as a global theological flow, liberation theologies deserve our attention in order to explore further under what conditions a universal theology might be pursued in the circumstances of our time.

Liberation theologians themselves have noted the changed circumstances under which liberation theologies are developed, but most reflections on what this means have been brief, until relatively recently.[1] There are some who continue to repeat the old formulas, mainly because poverty and misery continue to be present, and are even deepening for many. Others say that the single most important change in the context of theologies of liberation (at least in Latin America) is the unremitting repression of them by the Roman Catholic Church; the socioeconomic changes are less important.

The investigation of liberation theologies here will be under five headings. First, there will be a review of what has changed in the contexts and what are some of the consequences of those changes. For

---

[1]For shorter reflections, see Pablo Richard, "La Iglesia de los pobres en la decada de los noventos," *Pasos* 28 (1990): 10-19; "La teologia de la liberación en la nueva conyuntura," *Pasos* 34 (1991): 1-8. For longer, sustained reflections, see Juan José Tamayo, *Presente y futuro de la teologia de la liberación* (Madrid: San Pablo, 1994); José Comblin, *Cristãos rumo ao século XXI: Nova caminada de libertação* (São Paulo: Paulus, 1996). Comblin's rethinking is by far the most searching and thoroughgoing.

contextual theologies, one must begin with the context. Second, a survey of some of the possible directions that liberation theologies might take will be explored. The purpose of this survey is not to choose one direction over the others. After all, the diversity of contexts will require that different alternatives be utilized; moreover, different alternatives are frequently needed in the same context, given the strategy at any point in time. Third, one of the alternatives, namely, participation in the reconstruction of society, will be looked at in more detail. This alternative is chosen for special attention because of its importance in a number of places where there have been dramatic changes in the circumstances under which a theology of liberation has been developed, such as in South Africa, Chile, and the Philippines. It is also an alternative that a theology of liberation has not had the opportunity heretofore to pursue. Fourth, the theological task of liberation theologies will be reviewed in light of all of this, especially their brief to nourish utopian and prophetic thinking in situations of struggle by drawing upon Christian tradition. The biblical narrative of the Exodus and the biblical metaphor of the Reign of God have been central to this utopian and prophetic function in the past. Do other narratives and metaphors need to be called upon in changed times? Fifth and finally, the implications of what has happened to theologies of liberation will be reviewed briefly for what can be learned about global theological flows. If theologies of liberation truly are a species of universal theologies in a multicultural and pluralistic world, then reviewing how they have been changed will be instructive for other global theological flows.

Given the wide range—both conceptual and geographical—of theologies of liberation, it is not possible to include every type and every place here. In this chapter, emphasis will be placed on Latin America and South Africa: Latin America, because it is the birthplace of liberation theology and that region has undergone significant changes in recent years; South Africa, because of the legal end to apartheid and the efforts at reconciliation and the reconstruction of society taking place there.

I do not claim expertise in theologies of liberation and, as a North American, am an outsider to both locations. But as a frequent visitor to Latin America and as one who has tried in his own way to support developments there, I hope that what I have to say will make some contribution to the discussion.

CHANGES AND THEIR SIGNIFICANCE FOR A THEOLOGY OF LIBERATION

One needs to begin first of all by specifying what changes are significant in order to follow out the implications arising from them.

There are three changes that deserve special attention here. The first is the end of the socialist governments of Eastern Europe, beginning in 1989. The second is the end of apartheid and the move toward a reconstructed legal system and society in the Republic of South Africa. The third is the political and economic changes that have taken place in Latin America since 1985. Among those political changes are the transition from authoritarian military governments to some forms of democracy, the end of internecine warfare in Guatemala and El Salvador, the transition from Sandinista rule in Nicaragua, and the apparent quelling of the *sendero luminoso* in Peru. The economic changes involve the deeper incursion of neoliberal capitalism into Latin America, and the development of trading blocs such as Mercosur and NAFTA.

THE END OF SOCIALISM

The collapse of the socialist governments in Eastern Europe has undermined the credibility of at least one kind of socialism, and may have discredited socialism as a form of economy on a large scale altogether. While a number of socialist states still remain, socialism as a policy seems to be weakening in nearly all of them, or has become increasingly subordinate to nationalism (as in North Korea and, to some extent, in China). At any rate, the end of all these twentieth-century experiments with socialism has meant that there is at this time no economic alternative to capitalism, except in instances of small, relatively isolated, and self-sustaining communities. It is not the end of history, as has been trumpeted by some, but it is surely the end of a chapter in history. Socialism as a conceptual possibility has been brought into crisis, especially in its Leninist-Stalinist variety. Marxism as a whole has gone into eclipse as a result of the dramatic changes since 1989.

To be sure, socialism has gone through profound crises before, notably in the 1840s in Britain, when the last Owenite community died out; and in the first decade of the twentieth century in Germany and Russia, when it appeared that socialism would never achieve political power. In both instances, however, changes in circumstances led to a revival. Thus the news of socialism's demise may be greatly exaggerated. There is a good deal of work going on among economists scrutinizing possible socialist proposals and putting them forward tentatively, especially in Europe.[2] The crisis in socialism has pressed the critical appraisal of socialism in important ways, posing questions such as: Just

---

[2]See, for example, Frank Roosevelt and David Belkin (eds.), *Why Market Socialism?* (New York: M. E. Sharpe, 1994); Robin Archer, *Economic Democracy* (Oxford: Oxford University Press, 1995).

what is the "social" in socialism? What does the ownership of the means of production really mean and entail? What aspects of the economy are best left with the state? Socialism as a concept has not lost its allure. The widening gap between rich and poor under neoliberal capitalism, felt acutely in poor countries but now experienced also in wealthy countries, could lead eventually to widespread social upheaval. Alternatives to the varieties of current capitalism will be indispensable in mending the rent social fabric. In both *Sollicitudo Rei Socialis* and *Centesimus Annus*, Pope John Paul II has meditated on the strengths and weaknesses of both capitalism and socialism. And, neoconservative assertions notwithstanding, Roman Catholic social teaching seems tilted more in the direction of the goals (if not the reality) of socialism.

Marxism, while now in eclipse, is not likely to disappear entirely. Many of the tools of analysis that were developed under Marxist influence will continue to be with us. Some of them, of course—such as those that led to the conclusion that capitalism would soon collapse and socialism would triumph—are now seen to be superseded. As a *description* of systems of oppression, Marxism has much to teach. As a *prescription* for a new society, it is no longer likely to find many adherents. And, as has already been noted, dialectical thinking itself has become questionable.

What are the implications of the end of socialism for liberation theology? At the outset, it must be said that many liberation theologians, at least of the Latin American variety, were more anticapitalist than pro-socialist. Their principal concern was to identify and denounce the oppressive consequences of capitalism rather than to prescribe economic alternatives. Many chose not to make such prescriptions because they did not see that as the task of theologians—and there is some justification for such a stance. Their concern was for the dehumanizing consequences of capitalism as seen through the prism of the Gospel and Jesus' own way of life. Moreover, most liberation theologians would disavow the need for making such prescriptions because they were not trained in economics and political science.[3] There is some justification for this, but it is hardly total in nature. As some of their critics have pointed out, one cannot do adequate social analysis, let alone imagine alternatives, without engaging in some measure of economics and politics.[4] This is a point to which we shall return.

---

[3]An important exception is Franz Hinkelammert, who might be called a political economist with theological interests. Among the newest generation, see Brazilian theologian Jung Mo Sung, "Deus da vida e ídolo da morte na nova economia mundial," *Revista Eclesiástica Brasileira* 55 (1995): 838-50.

[4]See the discussion in Peter Burns, "The Problem of Socialism in Liberation Theology," *Theological Studies* 53 (1992): 493-516.

What the collapse of socialism has meant for liberation theology has been the loss of a horizon of utopia and prophecy.[5] Without such a horizon of utopia and prophecy it becomes very difficult to focus, mobilize, and sustain a struggle for a different kind of world. That different world must be able to be imagined, in however indistinct a fashion (and sometimes being indistinct has an advantage), in order for people to risk the present for the sake of a different kind of future. Revolution cannot live without utopia. Present evil can be denounced without a clear concept of an alternative good, but a praxis to eliminate the evil cannot be undertaken without some *telos*. Exodus from Egypt is not possible without the hope of a Promised Land; otherwise, it is only an exodus to die in the desert.

If some form of socialism is no longer a possibility, and neoliberal capitalism has now engulfed everything, is the struggle for liberation still possible? The apparent conquest by capitalism to the point that the only hope is exclusion from hope altogether has more than anything else prompted the crisis in liberation theology. The question becomes: what kind of alternative can now be imagined? Is the only possibility now, as Pablo Richard has opined, a struggle between good and evil, between light and darkness, that ends in apocalypse?[6] As we shall see, a major challenge for liberation theology is to imagine an alternative utopian horizon.

FROM APARTHEID TO DEMOCRACY

The second change has been the transition in South Africa from the rule of apartheid to democracy. The fact that the transition was made through democratic elections rather than a direct armed conflict and that subsequent developments have unfolded remarkably peacefully is for many a sign of God's grace in history. Today those who struggled for so long, exemplified especially in the figure of Nelson Mandela, now find themselves in positions of power.

Perhaps more in South Africa than anywhere else, a call is being made to move away from a posture of resistance to one of cooperation in the work of reconstructing a society. The experience of moving from resistance to reconstruction is a complex and even ambivalent one. On the one hand, there is the joy and the relief in attaining one's goal; the

---

[5]See Ignacio Ellacuría, "Utopia and Prophecy in Latin America," in Ignacio Ellacuría and Jon Sobrino (eds.), *Mysterium Liberationis: Fundamental Concepts of Liberation Theology* (Maryknoll, NY: Orbis Books, 1993), 289-327.

[6]Pablo Richard, "La teologia de la liberación en la nueva conyuntura," op. cit.; idem, *Apocalypse* (Maryknoll, NY: Orbis Books, 1995). But see also his "Pour un renouveau de la théologie de l'esperance," *SEDOS Bulletin* (1994) 233-38.

struggle that has been waged for so long meets its fulfillment. The achievement of the long-sought reality means that an alternative possibility now becomes real, the basis for a new kind of society. But solidarity in resistance is different from solidarity in the cooperation of reconstruction. As long as the struggle of resistance continues, the goal may remain indistinct or even abstract. "Freedom," for example, can be at once as concrete as release from prison and as abstract as a yet unknown state of being. Indistinctness allows many to be mobilized in the struggle without precise agreement on the nature of the goal. All energies can be poured into the task of the struggle. In reconstruction, the tasks are more intricate. They include coming to terms with the consequences of a violent past and the seeking of reconciliation. They involve building a new society upon the ruins of the old. In these tasks there will not be agreement on such issues as when reconciliation has taken place, when the past has been adequately confronted, and just what form the new society will take. A different kind of commitment is needed that involves patience, compromise, and cooperation. Progress is often not as marked as can be the case in resistance. Even when the object of resistance has fallen, much of the evil attendant upon it remains. Apartheid may no longer be tolerated, but its consequences linger on in disrupted social relations, or persist stubbornly in poverty and societal division. What will liberation theology have to say when it must move from resistance to programmatic proposals? Will it still be of use?

Most clearly in South Africa there have been calls for a theology of reconstruction coming from those who were prominent in the struggle against apartheid.[7] Charles Villa-Vicencio has suggested that the image of rebuilding the Temple upon return from Exile might be more appropriate than that of the Exodus for a theology of liberation in South Africa today. Returning from Exile is rich in possibility even as it is fraught with ambiguity. To what is one coming back? How have we changed in the midst of the struggle? And what should be (re)built? Not only in South Africa, but also in Eastern Europe and in the reunited Germany it is apparent that new societies do not spring full-blown from plans, like Athena from the head of Zeus. Synthesis does not follow upon antithesis so closely.

SOCIAL AND POLITICAL CHANGES IN LATIN AMERICA

The third area of change is in Latin America. Until recently, the majority of Latin American countries had military governments. At least

---

[7]Notably Charles Villa-Vicencio, *A Theology of Reconstruction: Nation-Building and Human Rights* (Cambridge: Cambridge University Press, 1992). See also

the veneer of democracy has been returned to these countries, since by the mid-1990s there were no military governments left on the continent. The collapse of socialism and communism has made itself felt throughout the region as well. Capitalism has made its inroads in new ways, with the economies of some countries, notably Brazil, Argentina, Chile, and Peru, expanding significantly. The Sandinista experiment, once the hope for many, has been voted out of office. Indeed, under democracy economically conservative leaders have been elected. This means that large numbers of those who are poor are voting for the policies that would appear to impoverish them even more. Why is this happening?

In the case of countries such as Peru, one might surmise that voting for Fujimori was voting for an alternative to what had been in place. To continue to return the PRI to power in Mexico would seem to indicate insufficient confidence in the alternatives. Whatever the case, events have produced disarray among leftist political parties and intellectuals.[8] In Catholic circles, the disintegration has been compounded by rightist pressure from the Church hierarchy, dismantling teaching and research institutes and discouraging base communities. The influx of conservative Protestant groups, especially from North America, has focused people on the personal rather than the social. In some places people are simply exhausted from the struggle to change things, so they turn away from engagement to bettering themselves and their families. And youth, once in the forefront of struggle in places like Chile, now turn to rock music, making money, and engaging in consumption of the global hyperculture.

In short, the changes that have been taking place in Latin America do not have the same clear profile found in South Africa or parts of Eastern Europe. The loss of horizon of utopia begins to look as though it has been replaced by the glitter of the global hyperculture. Even worse, there seems to be no basis for solidarity at all. Where, then, might liberation theology turn?

POSSIBLE DIRECTIONS FOR LIBERATION THEOLOGY

There are some who would say that liberation theologians do not need to turn anywhere. They should simply continue upon the trajectory that they have been following. The plight of the poor has not im-

---

J. N. K. Mugambi, *From Liberation to Reconstruction: African Christian Theology After the Cold War* (Nairobi: East African Educational Publishers, 1995).

[8]The best analysis of this situation available is Jorge Castaneda, *Utopia Unarmed: The Latin American Left Since the Cold War* (New York: Vintage, 1991).

proved. Indeed, freer entry of outside capital and corporations has actually worsened their plight in some areas. From the perspective of these poor, nothing has really changed; what has been the case has simply gotten worse. In this view, to change course in any way would betray the poor and break the solidarity that has been built up over three decades.

One can see the warrant for such a view. The massive consequences of poverty and misery still weigh heavily upon society. The fundamental vision of liberation still holds. Nevertheless, conditions are changing, although they are still riddled with ambivalence. There is evidence in Peru that significant portions of the informal economy are being integrated into the formal economy. That means, on the one hand, an increasing prosperity in those traditionally poor sectors, and an increased tax base for the nation. But it could mean, on the other, poising those newly integrated businesses for takeover and elimination by more powerful interests. On a more hopeful note, a portion of the new wealth in Chile is being channeled by the Frei government into restoring the social services curtailed under the Pinochet regime.

A NEW SOCIAL ANALYSIS?

One direction for liberation theology is to undertake a new social analysis. Such an analysis should try to account for more than why outside influences—be they global capitalism, the United States, the Roman Catholic Church, or the International Monetary Fund—have posed such a great challenge. These external factors are all very real. What are the factors internal to Latin American societies that account for poor populations voting for the right, for the embracing of Pentecostalism, and for the directions in which youth are moving? There is no clear picture on this yet, but Jorge Castaneda, as a political scientist, has made some suggestions, and José Comblin, as a theologian, has tried to do the same. Both are appreciative of liberation theology, but both question how deeply or widely it was ever able to move. They both question the extent to which the model of an elite serving as the vanguard of a new history served the poor. Castaneda provides a better understanding of the role of the intellectual in Latin American history and society. Comblin especially questions how well many liberation theologians really understood the dynamics and motivation of the poor. To provide the kind of analysis needed goes beyond the scope of this book and the competence of its author, but these two, Castaneda and Comblin, seem to be setting us in the right direction.[9] This is not to say

---

[9]Castaneda, op. cit., and Comblin, op. cit.

that liberation theologians have misread the poor. It is only to say that there must be a constant re-reading of the situation, and a willingness to use other forms of analysis, even when they go against cherished ways of seeing things.

REIMAGINING EVIL

A second possible direction involves reimagining the source of evil. For the last century and a half in Latin America, it has been the United States that has been seen as the source of evil. There has been ample evidence to support that claim. Anything coming from "el norte" was greeted with suspicion, a suspicion that was usually not disappointed. The exploitation and colonization of Latin America by the United States cannot be disputed. But there are also deep ambivalences. Central Americans have taken refuge in the United States from civil wars, and millions have entered the United States in search of work—so much so that Los Angeles is now the second largest city of Mexico, Guatemala, and Costa Rica; and Miami is the second largest city of Cuba, Panama, and Haiti.[10]

Part of this phenomenon is the migration of peoples already discussed above under globalization. Some Latin Americans have migrated to Australia and to Europe. But the large number of those who have migrated to the United States belies any belief in the uniformly evil character of the United States. Again, while not gainsaying the history of the evil that has come out of North America, two methodological points can be made about reimagining evil. First of all, concentration on the distant enemy—real as that enemy might be—may make one blind to the nearer one. Denouncing those who are far away is safer, and it also avoids the unpleasant fact that some measure of oppression comes from within. Second, concentrating on outside agents of evil can prolong the victimization of the colonized—a problem many Latin American thinkers have commented upon. It can undercut whatever sense of agency is emerging.

For example, when speaking of neoliberal capitalism as the source of oppression, it is worthwhile to remember that this is not a monolithic concept. There are varieties of capitalism, often in competition with one another. The ongoing trade struggle between the United States and Japan is evidence of that. Castaneda has proposed that Latin America can create a space for itself by playing off the various capitalisms (specifically, the Japanese, the American, and the German) against each

---

[10]Cited in "North of the Border: Origins and Fallacies of the 'Hispanic' Threat to the United States," *The Times Literary Supplement* (May 17, 1996) 15.

other.[11] Such nuancing may lose the value of indistinctness, but it does open up a strategy in the struggle against poverty and oppression.

A NEW UTOPIAN HORIZON?

On several occasions already in this chapter, it has been noted that a new utopian horizon is needed in the next stage of liberation theology. As we have seen, Pablo Richard has suggested apocalypse as a possibility. Others have suggested the vision of the Book of Ecclesiastes, whose author was singularly undazzled by the promises of Hellenistic culture for his occupied country, and who could assert that "those who increase knowledge increase sorrow" (1:18)—a powerful critique of an age of information.[12]

Still others have suggested, in the mode of a multipolar world, that this is not the time for grand visions. One should concentrate instead upon building up the intermediate structures of society, strengthening neighborhoods, urban zones, trade unions, and political parties.[13] Preoccupation with the political moves to the civil as the means of transformation of society. Comblin stresses especially working with youth. These suggestions conform well with the kind of world that globalization has created, where centers of power are no longer so clearly delineated, where network replaces hierarchy in communication, where multiple belonging is characteristic of a hybrid identity. This kind of world calls for living much more provisionally and patiently. If the Exodus provided a powerful impulse for the first generation of liberation theology, perhaps now the image is the sojourn in the desert. With it goes the watchfulness that Jesus enjoined upon his disciples—a watchfulness that is not just passive waiting, but one that is critical in its perception, one that can change its frame of perception to meet new possibilities.

A NEW DIFFERENTIATION IN THE AGENTS AND TASKS OF LIBERATION THEOLOGY

A fourth possible direction for liberation theology is to rethink the agents of liberation theology and its discrete tasks. In his consideration of the future of liberation theology, Juan José Tamayo suggests that in recent years liberation theologians have been rethinking the agents of

---

[11]Castaneda, op. cit., 431. The German model (which he calls the Rhineland model) would be typical of the social democracies of Western Europe, and is the one he prefers.

[12]I owe the insight into this use of the Wisdom literature to Ofelia Ortega.

[13]Castaneda, Comblin, and Richard ("La Teologia de la liberación en la nueva conyuntura," op. cit., 4-5) all make this point.

liberation theology. Already in the 1970s it was evident that the initial impulses of liberation theology had to be expanded to include both popular religion and spirituality. Today, it must include as subjects of their own history women, the indigenous, and those of African descent.[14]

One can also differentiate more clearly among the different tasks of liberation theology. By so doing one can indicate which is called for in a given situation. This coincides well with the intermediate-level approach outlined above. By differentiating the tasks, one sees better also the complexity of the tasks of liberation theology. There are at least five such tasks of liberation theology.

The first task is *resistance*. This involves the mobilization of those who are being oppressed to struggle against the sources of their oppression. In so doing, the oppressed become subjects of their own history, rather than passive agents locked in their fate. This is perhaps the best-known task of liberation theology. Although, as dictatorships or apartheid has receded, there has been a move beyond resistance on the national level in many countries, resistance continues to be necessary on many intermediate and local levels. Often this kind of struggle is necessary to maintain existence itself, and to give up the struggle is to give up life.

The second task is *denunciation*. This involves assuming the prophetic (and often dangerous) role of identifying and condemning the source of evil and oppression. Once it is named, that source can no longer disguise itself or pass itself off as simply the way things are. The 1985 Kairos Document in South Africa, which denounced church complicity in its acquiescence to apartheid, is an example of such denunciation. As was noted above, denunciation gives a face to evil, a way of imagining it that can lead to an engagement with it in struggle.

The third task is *critique*. Critique goes beyond denouncing the evil. It uncovers its ideological underpinnings and connections. It unmasks its power and how that power is maintained. And it shows how evil can spread itself through a society. The social analysis so central to liberation theology's method lays the groundwork for critique. As proposals are brought forward for a new society, these too benefit from critique.

The fourth task is *advocacy*. This takes the form of joining in solidarity in struggle or in the promotion of specific projects in specific areas. It was already seen that liberation must now be concentrated more on intermediate and local levels. Advocacy helps mobilize people and resources around those projects that will move the process forward.

---

[14]Tamayo, op. cit., 92-117.

The fifth task is *reconstruction*. Reconstruction identifies and acknowledges the kinds of change that have taken place in a situation and develops the means for new forms of cooperation. Reconstruction exhibits an awareness that it cannot be a return to the way things were in the past, since the past is irretrievably gone. But it reconstructs in the name of justice and in the hope for a renewed situation for humanity.[15]

To think in terms of discrete tasks within liberation theology is an acknowledgment that not everything can be done at once, and that circumstances may dictate focusing on one or more aspects of the enterprise at any given time. It is also an acknowledgment that not every situation calls for the same response. By so differentiating the tasks of liberation theology, its various parts can be highlighted and even strengthened.

RECONSTRUCTION

Hitherto the task of liberation theologians has essentially been to say 'No' to all forms of oppression. The prophetic 'No' must, of course, continue to be part of a liberating theology. As the enduring struggle for democracy in some parts of the world begins to manifest itself in different degrees of success, however, so the prophetic task of the church must include a thoughtful and creative 'Yes' to options for political and social renewal.[16]

Thus Charles Villa-Vicencio begins what he calls "a theology of reconstruction," an opportunity and a challenge to participate in the building of a just society on the ruins of apartheid in South Africa, built upon the very values that had been denied under apartheid to the great majority of South Africa's people. "As this *challenge* is met, *it could mean the birth of a different kind of theology*."[17] Reconstruction is a different kind of liberating theology, because the opportunity for it is so rare. As Villa-Vicencio makes clear, when the opportunity presents itself—be it in South Africa, Eastern Europe, Chile, Argentina, or elsewhere—it is a

---

[15]In the literature, an example of resistance would be Eleazar Fernandez, *Toward a Theology of Struggle* (Maryknoll, NY: Orbis Books, 1994); of denunciation, Jim Wallis, *The Soul of Politics* (Maryknoll, NY: Orbis Books, 1994); of critique, Juan Luis Segundo, *The Liberation of Theology* (Maryknoll, NY: Orbis Books, 1985); of advocacy, Jon Sobrino, *The Principle of Mercy* (Maryknoll, NY: Orbis Books, 1994); of reconstruction, Villa-Vicencio, op. cit.

[16]Villa-Vicencio, op. cit., 1.

[17]Ibid., 8 (his emphasis).

moment of grace that should not be bypassed. The question then arises as to how theology comes to participate in the reconstruction process. What theology might bring is a vision that can serve as a source of imagining a continual renewal of society. Borrowing from the work of J. H. Oldham from the 1930s, Villa-Vicencio sees this vision operating as a set of "middle axioms" that serve as provisional definitions of the society yet to be constructed, as evolving principles reshaped by the continuing encounter with an evolving society and tempered by the eschatological proviso that all social proposals work under—that only God brings the final fulfillment.[18]

The concept of middle axioms is a useful way to insert theology into a social process without wedding the Church or theology to a single outcome. It brings to bear the power of the Gospel without making it beholden to any one situation. Villa-Vicencio sees collaboration in interdisciplinary work paired with the concept of middle axioms as another point of engagement for a theology of reconstruction. In the situation of South Africa, where the legal structure of apartheid has had to be replaced, law and human rights have become the natural place for such collaboration, and Villa-Vicencio's book is devoted to that interdisciplinary collaboration. The outcome, it is hoped, will be truly liberating for South African society.

These two principles—seeking middle axioms and discovering points of interdisciplinary collaboration—map out a procedure for a theology of reconstruction. Identifying where the Gospel needs to be heard in a society undergoing reconstruction and locating the disciplines or policies that should be influenced provide a way to engage a society without theology's foregoing its prophetic edge and offers a vehicle whereby the Good News can be truly liberating.

If one turns to other contemporary situations, one can suggest additional places where middle axioms might be operative. Ernest Gellner, for example, proposed that, where societies are being reconstructed after authoritarian rule (he had Eastern Europe in mind), it is *civil society* that must be concentrated upon.[19] Authoritarian rule tends to break down any mediating structures between itself and direct surveillance of the individual. The mediating structures are clubs, associations, and voluntary institutions. The task of civil society is to rebuild such structures, for they humanize a society by providing ways for people to be sociable and altruistic. Religion typically provides many of these kinds of associations. We have seen the power of them in the base communi-

---

[18]Ibid., 9.

[19]Ernest Gellner, *Conditions of Liberty: Civil Society and Its Rivals* (London: Hamish Hamilton, 1994).

ties in Latin America, suspected there too by authoritarian hierarchs. Gellner's suggestion points the way for a theology of reconstruction in Eastern Europe.

In a similar mode, Fernando Castillo, in surveying the crisis of socialism in Latin America, suggested that modernization is the key to liberation. Modernization would take its own specific form in Latin America, but would involve democracy (especially at the local or popular level), and would be expressed especially in small, sustainable projects of education, health, and community organization rather than grand strategies. Latin America is at an axial moment, and modernization is the basis upon which any progress might be built.[20]

Writing in greater detail and in a more pragmatic than visionary mode, Jorge Castaneda has suggested that Latin American nations strike a "grand bargain" with the wealthy nations of the North for reconstruction, offering a proposal that will not be entirely palatable to them, but more attractive than a possible scenario of social upheaval, disruption, and migration. If a bargain is not struck, the processes of globalization will facilitate the closing of Latin American markets to Northern suppliers and flood the North's cities with economic migrants. To make the grand bargain possible, Latin America will have to reform itself as well, sending down deeper roots of democracy and changing its own tax base so as to provide additional money for social spending. Like Castillo and Gellner, he advocates strengthening what he calls mid-level structures.[21]

To those immersed in previous theologies of liberation, a theology of reconstruction may seem more like a surrender to capitalism than an alternative to it. But in a time of eclipse for socialism, one needs to ask: what are the goals to which socialism aspires, and how might its values be incorporated into the reconstruction of societies when opportunities present themselves? Given the fact of growing populations, one must ask questions about how to create wealth as well as how to distribute it. Were the current wealth in Latin America distributed more evenly, poverty would likely still not disappear.

Just as there are a variety of socialisms to be imagined, so too there are different social arrangements that can be made within capitalism. Castaneda himself favors what he calls "the Rhineland" model, based on the economic system of the Federal Republic of Germany, with agreements struck between labor and capital and a wide range of social

---

[20]Fernando Castillo, "Teologia y liberación en los noventa: Un análisis de la conyuntura latinoamericana," *Freiburger Zeitschrift für Philosophie und Theologie* 39 (1992): 391-423.
    [21]Castaneda, op. cit., 427-76.

services. A blanket demonization of capitalism is not useful here, and may run the risk of missing the opportunity of an axial moment.

THE THEOLOGICAL TASK

What then is the theological task for a theology of liberation, given the changed circumstances? On the basis of what has been said thus far, four things come to mind. A social analysis, of course, is presumed.

First of all, liberation theology needs to determine what mode of response is appropriate and most effective in its setting. Is it resistance, saying a profound "no" to a situation, and mobilizing others into that "no"? Is it prophetic denunciation, pointing a finger at the evil and not allowing it to be varnished over as "inevitable" or "necessary"? Or are there new proposals being offered that call for an ideological critique? Is advocacy of certain groups and projects now in order? Or is there an axial moment of opportunity now opening up that makes collaboration in reconstruction a possibility? Again, more than one mode of response may be needed in any given situation. But this kind of differentiation allows a theology of liberation to lead with its strength, rather than getting into a dispute about which mode is the genuine or authentic liberation theology.

Second, liberation theology needs to explore the Scriptures and subsequent tradition to find the images and narratives that give rise to utopian vision and hope. The image of the Reign of God and the narrative of the Exodus have provided that utopian vision for many. But new images and narratives may serve better in changed circumstances. Villa-Vicencio has suggested the return from Exile and the rebuilding of Jerusalem as narratives to provide the horizon for reconstruction. In South Africa the biblical concept of reconciliation has also been suggested.[22] Reconciliation's horizon of the New Creation (2 Cor 5:17) may serve societies in reconstruction as well as in dealing with ecological concerns. When exploring images and narratives, it must be remembered that every image and narrative can be read from different perspectives, leading sometimes to opposing meanings. The Exodus story was not Good News to Native Americans or to Palestinians, who had their land taken away by the invaders. Nor is it liberating to contemporary Coptic Christians under pressure from the Egyptian govern-

---

[22]There are problems with introducing reconciliation as an overarching theme in Latin America. This is because reactionary Church forces tried to co-opt the concept as an alternative to liberation. See "Declaración de los Andes," *Mensaje* 34 (1985): 399-402 for the text of the statement that tried to launch this effort.

ment—Exodus would mean exile. Nonetheless, within the polyvalent character of biblical images and narratives, resources for new utopian visions can be found.

Third, middle axioms—provisional definitions of the human and of a just society to which the message of the Gospel can contribute—need to be sought out. For Villa-Vicencio, middle axioms were to be found in the new legal structure that would have embedded in it the very values that apartheid had denied. For others, such axioms could be found in the values of community and solidarity present in civil society. Middle axioms provide concrete points of reflection and insertion into society, points at which moments of grace might well up.

Fourth, liberation theologies must be ready to become more interdisciplinary, especially in situations of reconstruction. While it may be protested that it is not theology's task to provide concrete proposals for the reconstruction of society, a theology truly arising from and grounded in praxis cannot avoid this kind of concreteness. There is a difference, it seems to me, between getting identified with a single proposal (something that theology probably should not do), and foregoing the hard work of sorting through the vexing issues that make up reality. There is a place in liberation theology for prophetic denunciation. There is also a place for engaged, interdisciplinary work in matters of reconstruction.

In sum, then, liberation theology is called to a number of challenges in this changed world. Its time has by no means passed; there is still much for it to do. Still, adjustments have to be made as it refocuses its efforts. Its proponents are correct: the issues surrounding poverty and oppression are still very much with us. But our mode of response must be commensurate with the changed conditions under which the world now operates.

GLOBAL THEOLOGICAL FLOWS

Global theological flows were discussed in the first chapter, and then at the beginning of this one. They were defined as an interlocking set of mutually intelligible discourses that together make up an antisystemic global movement. It was suggested that they may be the form of "universal" theology in a globalized world, for they address global systems (in the case of liberation theology, the global economic system) and interlink responses to it. They may not be universal in the transcendental sense, but they achieve a certain universality on the basis of their sheer pervasiveness.

We may recall that Peter Beyer saw them as posing a theological answer to an economic question. After this examination of the future of liberation theology in the space between resistance and reconstruction, one sees the possibility for a more nuanced picture of liberation and, perhaps, of global theological flows in general. While global theological flows may not have engaged (in this case) in economic questions directly, that does not mean that they are completely unlinked from the global economic reality. The fact is that as the global economic system changed with the collapse of socialism, so too liberation theologies have undergone a change. Moreover, with the option of engaging in reconstruction, the possibility of a new interdisciplinary approach opens up for the first time. Observing how liberation theologies reconfigure themselves in the coming years, then, will teach us something about global theological flows themselves and how they provide a kind of universal theology in our world today.

7

The New Catholicity

A LOOK BACK

As this book comes to its conclusion, it would be worthwhile to recall what prompted the exploration of the theme of theology between the global and the local in the first place, and where we have come in this investigation. There has been a great deal of intense reflection and communication about theology and its contexts in recent years, especially in the form of working out concrete theological expressions in quite specific contexts. At the same time, the collapse of the bipolar world system has brought about a new awareness of ethnicity in Asia and Europe. The 1992 quincentennial celebration of the arrival of Christopher Columbus in the Americas created a similar awareness among native peoples in the Americas. And throughout the world there has been an increasing interest in the local, be it in the form of tourism or nostalgia, a hearkening back to an imagined past with more holism and harmony than the present.

The Roman Catholic Church, at the level of official discourse, encouraged inculturation, especially for those small-scale societies who were minorities struggling to maintain their identities in larger populations. But the complaint kept coming from many quarters that very little actual inculturation was being permitted, and so the rhetoric of inculturation was beginning to sound more and more hollow.

Seeing such paradoxes leads one naturally to wonder what underlying concerns have led to a greater interest in the local on the one hand and an apparent fear of it on the other. But before addressing how all of this might best be theorized, there are some questions about universalizing, contextual, and liberation theologies to be reviewed.

First of all, if contextual theologies had begun in reaction to the universalizing theologies of the West, would they always maintain a somewhat marginal status over against those universalizing theologies, as some of their critics would maintain? Were they of such a local nature that one could not generalize from them? An interesting development is that in recent years contextual theologies began to be of interest to those in the West who were part of the mainstream of their respective cultures. Contextual theologies spread to those areas where another kind of theology was already being intensely cultivated. Some of the reasons for this development were explored in chapter 5. What does this say about the status of contextual theologies today?

A second, related question has to do with the status of contextual theologies vis-à-vis theologies of liberation. It is clear that these two kinds of theology had always been close to each other, frequently growing up in the same local environments. But contextual theologies had a preference for coming to a deeper understanding of identity, in order to overcome what has been called in Africa an "anthropological poverty."[1] Anthropological poverty grew out of the violence of colonization, in which local people were stripped of their identities or made to feel ashamed of them. The restoration and reconstruction of identity was therefore of paramount importance. There is clearly also an awareness of social ills and other forms of oppression among contextual theologians. Some, like Bénézet Bujo, call special attention to social ills and oppression, and make a point of urging that they be taken into consideration in contextual theologies.[2] But the methods of investigation favored the investigation of culture more than that of current social problems.

Liberation theologies, on the other hand, focused especially on social transformation. Their methods of analysis sought to uncover patterns of oppression so as to mobilize communities to struggle against them. To be sure, they took up issues of identity as well, especially in their efforts to help the poor and the oppressed become subjects of their own history. The people to whom liberation theologies were directed often were the very same people to whom contextual theologies were directed. If one follows the CELAM statements from Medellín through Puebla to Santo Domingo, one sees an ever increasing interest in culture, due in large part to the struggles of native peoples in Latin America.

Just as contextual theologies were not only for non-Western people, so also liberation theologies began to be developed for mainstream-culture Europeans and North Americans, although these at-

---

[1] The phrase was first used by Camerounian theologian Engelbert Mveng.

[2] See his *African Theology in Its Social Context* (Maryknoll, NY: Orbis Books, 1992).

tempts were generally not very successful. An even greater challenge came with the passing of the bipolar world system which, with the end of socialism, discouraged thinking about an economic alternative to the neoliberal capitalism that was now regnant everywhere and was so oppressive to the poor.

The changed circumstances of all three of these kinds of theology—universalizing, contextual, and liberation—called out for a new way of thinking about them.

Another set of concerns were raised in interpretation and communication. Advances in communications technologies were changing the way people communicate and relate. Questions of intercultural communication and hermeneutics, the concept of culture itself, and the coming together of cultures in identity-forming processes that some call syncretism and others call synthesis had to be added to the questions about theology.

In short, all of these areas needed to be theorized in a new kind of way. This was especially the case because identity and social conflict were frequently paired together in ethnification processes, as contexts were being destabilized by mass and electronic communication as well as migration, resulting in peoples being thrown together into close proximity in an unprecedented fashion. The way to imagine this was not a New World Order or the end of history. If anything, a new world disorder was emerging.

The theory that held the most promise for accounting for all of this, and not just from the viewpoint of the wealthy minority or the poor majority separately, was globalization theory. But even globalization theory tends to address the issues principally from the perspective of the wealthy minority. It was therefore supplemented in this discussion by postcolonial criticism, since it offers a significant voice to the culturally displaced and oppressed populations at this point in history.

A revised globalization theory can account for the positioning of the various kinds of theology and explain why interest in the local has increased and why liberation theologies face new challenges. It also offers ways of understanding religious identity formation and religious movements—especially fundamentalisms and ethnifications—and the roles they play in the world today. Viewing liberation theologies and other forms of theological critique as global theological flows, we get a glimpse of what is a new type of universalizing theology.

What remains to be done is to bring globalization theory itself into closer dialogue with theology, by finding concepts in theology that globalization can inform but not determine. Theology must be able to interact with globalization theory out of its own internal history and resources and not be simply reactive to it. It seems to me that the concept of *catholicity* may be the theological concept most suited to developing a theological view of theology between the global and the local in a world Church.

MARKS OF THE CHURCH AND THEIR HISTORY

To invoke catholicity is to invoke one of the "marks" or defining characteristics of the Church, enunciated by the Council of Constantinople in its addition to the Nicene Creed: "[and in] one, holy, catholic, and apostolic church." The marks of the Church have had a very uneven history in theology. They have varied in number (from two to one hundred), designation, and purpose.[3] Yet from their long history, a number of points can be culled that are significant for the discussion here.

First of all, reflection on the marks of the Church is usually at its keenest in times of change, conflict and transition. As postcolonialist writer Robert J. C. Young reminds us, "Fixity of identity is only sought in situations of instability and disruption, of conflict and change."[4] Over the course of history, the marks of the Church have been invoked and emphasized at moments of conflict about the self-understanding of the Church. Optatus and Augustine invoked the marks of unity and holiness in their disputes with the Donatists. The Cathari and other medieval movements questioned the holiness of the Church as well. The controversies over the reform of the Church from the fifteenth to the seventeenth centuries questioned the medieval Church's apostolicity: had it lost its connection to the Church of the Apostles? A somewhat similar questioning can be found in the Church of England in the nineteenth century among the Tractarians.

It is not surprising, then, that in the time of the emergence of the World Church we might examine more closely the nature of its catholicity, in what way it is *kath'holon*, throughout the whole.

Second, although reflection on the marks of the Church has generally occurred in situations of conflict and controversy, the struggles have been of an intrachurch nature. They have been between competing groups within the one Church, each claiming to be the true manifestation of the Church of Jesus Christ. But even when used in this intrachurch fashion, there have been theologians who have maintained

---

[3]For an historical overview and literature, see Peter Steinacker, "Katholizität," *Theologische Realenzyklopädie*, vol. 18, 72-80.

[4]Robert J. C. Young, *Colonial Desire: Hybridity in Theory, Culture and Race* (London: Routledge, 1995), 4.

their empirical, public, and verifiable nature, there for all rational people to see and to judge for themselves.

Such intrachurch usage of the marks of the Church might seem to
disqualify them from this more public discussion. But the issue of their
public nature raises an important point, particularly in relation to the
mark of catholicity. If the mark of catholicity is defined in an empirical, public, and verifiable way, then a far greater number of people can
participate in the debate, both within and outside the Church, as to its
nature and the conditions of its verifiability. This underscores the concept of meaning established above on the basis of intercultural communication theory, that both speaker and hearer enter into intense dialogue
in order to establish the meaning of a communication. Given that any
discussion of catholicity will involve discourse across many cultural
boundaries within a world Church, intercultural communication and
hermeneutics will have to be attended to. Discussion of the mark of
catholicity, then, cannot be solely an intrachurch debate, nor one restricted to elites in the Church.

Third, since at least the sixteenth century, the marks have been
construed in such a way that, once they are established as marks, they
could lead deductively to the discovery of the true Church. Does this
procedure go against the contextual and inductive methods favored by
both contextual and liberation theologies?

If the marks are used in a historical fashion, one would have to
agree. But what if a mark were used as a heuristic concept instead, to
open up both a fresh reading of the mark and a critical rereading of the
situation which has destabilized identity? Or what if the mark were used
as an eschatological limit-concept toward which the Church grows? It
would seem that marks need not be restricted to deductive uses.[5]

Thus, one must modify to some extent how a theology of the
marks has been developed and used historically. The purpose here is
not so much to test the authenticity of an ecclesial body as to come to a
heuristic understanding of what catholicity means now that the Church
is extended throughout the world and is committed to inculturation in
diverse places.

Before exploring that heuristic possibility, it might be good to recall briefly the history of the term "catholicity."[6] The term first ap-

---

[5]This is discussed in further detail in Robert Schreiter, "Marks of the Church
in Times of Transformation," in Letty M. Russell (ed.), *The Church with AIDS: Renewal in the Midst of Crisis* (Louisville, KY: Westminster/John Knox Press, 1990),
122-32.

[6]See Steinacker, op. cit., and Yves Congar, "Die Katholizität der Kirche," in J.
Feiner and M. Lohrer (eds.), *Mysterium Salutis: Grundriss heilsgeschichtlicher
Dogmatik* (Einsiedeln: Benziger, 1972), vol. 4/1, 478-502.

pears with Ignatius of Antioch around the year 110: "Wherever the bishop appears, there let the people be; as wherever Jesus Christ is, there is the catholic church" (*Smyr* 8, 2). Scholars have debated whether "catholic" here refers to the Church's universality or to its orthodoxy. However Ignatius is interpreted, it was to be around these two poles, universality and orthodoxy (in the sense of the *pleroma* or fullness of faith) that the meanings of catholicity would come to circulate. In the latter sense, catholicity came to be associated with the orthodox rule of faith, that is to say, the faith that was believed and professed everywhere.

Catholicity took on increasingly geographic overtones as Christianity spread and eventually came to be accepted as the religion of the Roman Empire. Just as the Empire embraced the *oikumene*, the entire inhabited world, so too the Church was seen as ecumenical, reaching to the ends of the earth. This reaching to the ends of the earth has to be understood symbolically, since other peoples were of course known to exist beyond the borders of the Empire. But these lay outside the civilized world of the *civitas romana*.

The increased status of the See of Rome brought with it a juridical sense to the meaning of catholic. To be a Catholic, at least in the Latin West, was to be in communion with Rome. The juridical sense was strengthened throughout the Middle Ages and reached a crucial moment at the time of the Reformation. After the Reformation the Church of Rome increasingly understood catholicity as referring to a uniformity achieved by communion with the bishop of Rome, the pope. Under the pressures of republicanism and nationalism in the nineteenth century, Pope Pius IX brought to the concept of catholicity the additional attribute of immutability.

But alongside this more juridical sense of catholicity, a mystical sense of the concept perdured in the Eastern Church,[7] a position taken over by churches of the Reformation. Catholicity here meant the fullness of the Church that would be achieved only at the end of time. The Church's catholicity would be revealed in heaven. The Church visible is incomplete and broken, but already participates in the Church invisible, as it is drawn into heaven by its Lord.

This brief sketch shows that catholicity has had many meanings: of fullness and orthodoxy, of extendedness and even identification with Empire, of juridical bond and conformity, of the partial and visible manifestation of the completeness and to-be-revealed lordship of

---

[7]For an account of the Orthodox point of view, see John H. Erickson, "The Local Churches and Catholicity: An Orthodox Perspective," *The Jurist* 52 (1992): 490-508.

Christ. As circumstances under which people lived their lives changed, so too did their sense of the catholicity of the Church. Today, members of the Church of Rome still see "catholic" as the most distinctive part of their name. Orthodox claim it too, as do some Anglicans and Lutherans in their self-identification. Nearly all Christians would claim to be part of the "Church catholic" (as opposed to the "Catholic Church"). One approach to exploring catholicity or the catholic meaning of the Church is to examine how the Church understands itself in the world in which it lives. It is to that world that we now turn.

THE CHURCH AND ITS CONTEXTS AS A BASIS
FOR A NEW CATHOLICITY

To understand what catholicity means in a globalized world, we must trace the broad outlines of how catholicity might be viewed in the Church-world relationship. The previous section looked at internal understandings of catholicity: what catholicity has meant inside the Church. This section traces self-understandings vis-à-vis the world. Put another way, we are looking at the Church's *mission*, in a twofold sense: how the Church sees its purpose in and for the world, and (from a more theological point of view) how the Church understands evangelization.

We will scan the period from the beginning of European empire to the present, that is, from the end of the fifteenth century through the end of the twentieth. This corresponds with Wallerstein's somewhat longer view of the period of the globalization of the world economy,[8] the beginning of modernity, and the beginning of the worldwide communication that has been sustained down to the present time. (Earlier periods of such outreach, from Greece under Alexander the Great, or later out of China, were not sustained. Moreover, these earlier instances of outreach did not include the Americas or Australia.) There are three discernible periods in those five hundred years of history of the Church's mission and they help illumine the current situation in which the world finds itself.

To help see the unfolding of the church's relation to the world in each of the three phases, I would propose four categories to guide the survey and serve as a basis for comparison of the three periods. The first category is the *carrier*, an image or metaphor or concept that is emblematic of where society sees itself going. This carrier is actualized

---

[8] Immanuel Wallerstein, *The Modern World System: Capitalist Agriculture and the Origins of the European World-Economy in the Sixteenth Century* (New York: Academic Press, 1974).

in the form of *universality*—the second category—that forms the horizon of self-understanding for the society. Religion responds to this universality by translating it into theological language. This constitutes the third category, the *theological mode*. The actualization of the theological mode is the fourth and final category, the understanding of *mission*. As with all such schemes, it distorts the complexities of reality because of its need to simplify. But it can also give us a way of conceptualizing previous experience and positioning ourselves to understand the present even as we gaze into the immediate future.[9]

THE PERIOD OF EXPANSION (1492–1945)

The first phase of the Church's missionary activity extends from the time of the voyages of European discovery at the turn of the fifteenth century to the end of the Second World War—the period of European empire. This was the period in which Europe expanded into all the other continents of the world, creating empires and colonies on an unprecedented scale. This was also the period of the rise of a new economic form, capitalism, which allowed for the creation of wealth rather than merely a redistribution of it. To be sure, there was a considerable redistribution as well—mainly from the colonial periphery to the imperial center. But capitalism as an engine for the creation of wealth confounded that Malthusian prediction that population would outstrip food resources. Capitalism in the nineteenth century also spawned its opposite, socialism, which sought to be a more humane and harmonious alternative to an often brutal and perpetually unstable capitalism.

The image that was the carrier of this period was *expansion*. The world was imagined as something to be discovered and claimed. As is now so clear in retrospect, that discovering and claiming was done from a very narrow perspective—that of the adventuresome and not infrequently greedy European. Expansion looks different if it is one's own culture that is being invaded. The mode of universality that actualized expansion was *civilization*. Civilization provided both a universalizing view that unified the purposes and goals of life, and the justification for invading other lands and claiming them as one's own. The people that the Europeans were encountering in the Americas and later in Africa "needed" European civilization, for they were deemed inferior to the Europeans, because they were either possessed by demons or

---

[9]This has been worked out in slightly different form in Robert Schreiter, "The Theological Meaning of a Truly Catholic Church," *New Theology Review* 7 (November, 1994): 5-14.

were still children culturally.[10] Europeans had a "duty" to bring their civilization to these natives and savages, these children of nature.

The Church's theological response to this vision of expansion was *world mission*. Like the expanding empires, the Church saw its task as expanding its own boundaries in the *plantatio ecclesiae*. Just as the empire builders had to civilize, so the Church had to save souls, engaging in the *conversio animarum*. These two concepts, the *plantatio ecclesiae* and the *conversio animarum*—the planting of the church and the conversion of souls—circumscribed the Church's sense of mission. Not dissimilar from the internal effects that empire had on the kingdoms of Europe, the identity of the Church, its mission, became tied up for the first time with coordinated and planned expansion. Evangelization had been carried on before, but generally in a decentralized and sometimes haphazard way. The new sense of mission developed first in those kingdoms of Europe that were involved in empire-building, and grew to its highest point in the nineteenth century when all of Western Europe was scrambling to acquire colonies. It was in this period that so many mission societies, both Protestant and Catholic, were founded. It was also in this period that Matthew 28:19-20, the so-called Great Commission, came to be invoked as the reason for the Church's existence.[11]

To say all of this is not to equate the Church's sense of world mission in this period with empire-building. Missionaries often sided with colonized peoples against the colonizers. And many Protestant mission-sending societies (and later on, the Vatican) urged autonomy and self-governance by the colonial churches early on. But one would be hard put to explain the sudden burst of coordinated activity without the imperial movement in Europe.

The first phase continued into the middle of the twentieth century. The Great War of 1914–1918 was the beginning of the end for empire, and the Second World War sealed its fate. During the same time, changes were afoot in the Church's understanding of mission.

THE PERIOD OF SOLIDARITY (1945–1989)

The second phase begins after 1945 and continues to 1989. It is the period of the bipolar world of the Cold War, of capitalism versus socialism, with the poor majority of the world's peoples oscillating be-

---

[10]See Bernard McGrane, *Beyond Anthropology: Society and the Other* (New York: Columbia University Press, 1989); Tzvetan Todorov, *The Conquest of America* (New York: Harper and Row, 1984).

[11]This is traced back to the Lutheran missionary Justinian von Welz (1621–1668).

tween the two. After the Second World War, the empires that had been built up over the previous period were dismantled or reconfigured into networks of economic cooperation. Between the late 1940s and 1970, region after region was given independence and new nation-states were set up, although independence—economically, at least—was often illusory. In this same period, from 1945 into the mid-1970s Europe and North America experienced rapid economic expansion. The carrier of this second phase was *growth* and *development*. The idea was that the industrialized countries of the world would continue to grow economically and would give of their surplus wealth to the poor nations to encourage economic development there. In the process the newly independent nations would recover the identity lost in colonialism and transcend ethnic differences to become nation-states. There would be a real "progress of peoples," to echo the title of Pope Paul VI's 1967 encyclical letter. The actualization of this carrier of growth and development, its mode of universality, was *optimism*: the evils of the past really could be overcome by continued economic growth and development. The stirring of youth in Europe and North America in the late 1960s seemed only to confirm this optimism.

On the religious side there were new configurations of this sense of growth and development in a horizon of optimism. Churches of the Reformation and of Orthodoxy came together in the World Council of Churches, which had ambitious plans of coming to a new Church unity. The Roman Catholic Church abandoned the fortress mentality against the modern world that it had assumed in the nineteenth century, and embraced that same modern world in the Second Vatican Council. Its optimism was perhaps most evident in the Pastoral Constitution on the Church in the Modern World, *Gaudium et Spes*, that appeared toward the end of the Council. Relationships between the older churches of Europe and the churches of the former colonies underwent changes as well. Voices from the South, joined by liberal voices in the North, called into question the heretofore predominant theological mode of universality, world mission. The concept was seen as so closely allied to colonialism as to be irredeemable. There were calls for a moratorium on sending any more missionaries from the North. There was, finally, a fundamental questioning of the value of mission itself. For the mainline churches, both Protestant and Catholic, the mode of mission of the first period had clearly run its course.

All of these changes were incubating in the larger crucible of society, with development as its carrier and optimism as its mode of universality. The theological response resonated with this larger picture. For Catholics, the Second Vatican Council unleashed great optimism. Many predicted dramatic changes on all ecclesiastical fronts within a few years. Theologies of hope blossomed across Western Europe. Dialogue seemed to supplant proclamation as the form of mission on many fronts: dialogue among the churches, dialogue with Marxist humanists in Western Europe, and dialogue with other great religious traditions. The image of world religious leaders coming together to pray for peace at Assisi in 1986 is emblematic of those times.

A concept that started to emerge in the late 1970s captured the mood of this phase and names the theological mode of universality: *solidarity*. Rather than the older churches giving something and the younger churches receiving it, North and South would now walk side by side. After the scathing criticisms and calls for moratoria in world mission in the 1960s and 1970s, by 1980 a new form of mission was emerging. It saw mission as dialogue, inculturation, and liberation—three forms of solidarity.[12] The churches were called upon to work together in equality, mutuality, and commitment. Language coming out of Latin America during this period seemed best to define this new sense of mission in solidarity: *promoción*, or advancement; *inserción*, or commitment to enter into the lives of the poor; *acompañamiento*, or walking side by side, rather than leading and following; and *liberación*, the struggle for a better and more just life, freed from poverty and oppression. If the biblical warrant for mission in the first period was the Great Commission, in this period it was Luke 4:18-19. The results of these modes of solidarity would be a new mutuality or communion among the churches, committed to authenticity in inculturation and to justice in liberation.

THE PERIOD OF GLOBALIZATION (1989–)

It has been said that the twentieth century began in August, 1914 with the Great War in Europe. It could equally be said that it ended in 1989 with the fall of the Berlin Wall. But the conditions leading up to 1989 had begun much earlier. The OPEC oil embargo is often seen as marking the time when economic power and the concomitant modes of production began to shift. New technologies, especially in communication, began to move the wealthiest economies away from being based on heavy industry to a new basis in information, high technology, and services. This new reality, which was explored extensively in the first chapter, is captured in the concept of globalization.

The carrier of this new reality is *global capitalism*. The virtual collapse of socialism as an alternative has been accompanied by this new

---

[12]These three emerged as forms of mission, along with proclamation, out of the 1981 SEDOS Seminar in Rome. See Joseph Lang and Mary Motte (eds.), *Mission in Dialogue* (Maryknoll, NY: Orbis Books, 1982), 633-649.

form of capitalism characterized by the mobility and flexibility of capital, information, and other resources rather than the building up of large corporations and industrial bases. It is characterized further by postnationalism (political boundaries lose their importance, and new economic associations blur national identities further), network rather than hierarchy in communication, a polycentric view of the world, and an acceleration of pace that makes short-term the only acceptable time span. It is bringing new wealth and opportunities for some, but for even more it is creating a new immiseration, conflict, uncertainty, and a sense of no alternatives for those not included in the global flow of information, technology, capital, and goods.

The mode of universality in this globalizing reality is lodged in *communication*, signified in communications technology. Those who have access to this technology may participate in the globalized reality and the power it brings. It operates by network rather than hierarchy, and is characterized by the compression of time and space. The communication occurs also in a global hyperculture, wherein signifiers of consumption (cola drinks, denim jeans, rock music, and video entertainment) are drawn largely from American culture and circulated worldwide. This hyperculture is then received into local cultures, often in different ways, creating homogeneity on the one hand, and provoking new intensifications of the local on the other.

What becomes the theological response to this third phase? To be sure, the theological responses from the previous phases retain valence. Mission as understood in the first and second phases still holds a certain validity. But it is noteworthy that some of the prime theological responses of the second phase have increasingly encountered difficulties: ecumenism appears to stagnate; the possibility of genuine dialogue with the other is questioned; inculturation does not seem to be advancing; and liberation loses some of its power as it confronts a world in which there is no alternative to neoliberal capitalism. The problems the second phase addressed have not gone away, but, since they are now framed differently by a change in their contexts, their solutions seem less efficacious.

TOWARD A NEW CATHOLICITY

It seems to me that a renewed and expanded concept of catholicity may well serve as a theological response to the challenge of globalization. It can provide a theological framework out of which the Church might understand itself and its mission under changed circumstances. Faced with the diversity of cultures and the implications of taking them seriously, and the challenge of maintaining the unity and integrity of the Church worldwide, the eschatological sense of catholicity, so important to the Orthodox and many Protestant churches, and reaffirmed by Roman Catholics at the Second Vatican Council,[13] takes on new salience at the interface of the global and the local. This is echoed in some reflections on catholicity: Avery Dulles speaks of catholicity as the ability to hold things together in tension with one another; Peter Schineller speaks of it as a tentativeness, anticipating the whole.[14]

Siegfried Wiedenhofer has expressed aptly what needs to be added to the traditional understanding of catholicity as extension throughout the world and orthodoxy in faith. He defines catholicity as "wholeness and fullness through exchange and communication."[15] "Wholeness" refers to the physical extension of the Church throughout the world; "fullness," to orthodoxy in faith. "Through exchange and communication" corresponds to the mode of universality in the third phase described above, communication. In a world where communication, information, and knowledge so define the landscape, it is vital that the Church incorporate communication more consciously in its sense of catholicity. The symbolic sense of communication has been understood by Pope John Paul II, who has utilized modern transportation to traverse the world so as to maintain unity in the Roman Catholic Church and to acknowledge its diversity. What needs now to be added is a stronger sense of intercultural communication and its meaning for culture itself. Let us examine what a new catholicity means in all three of its aspects of wholeness, fullness, and exchange and communication.

A NEW WHOLENESS

First, then, let us look at wholeness as an aspect of a new catholicity. One must posit a certain commensurability of cultures, in the sense that all cultures may receive the Word of God and be able in some measure to communicate with one another, despite real and legitimate differences. If there are cultures that are not capable, in their basic codes, of receiving and transmitting God's revelation—cultures that can be saved only by being destroyed—or if cultures are in some instances finally incommensurate, then one must give up either the uni-

---

[13]*Lumen Gentium*, 13.

[14]Avery Dulles, *The Catholicity of the Church* (Oxford: The Clarendon Press, 1985); Peter Schineller, "Inculturation as a Pilgrimage to Catholicity," *Concilium* 204 (1989): 98-106.

[15]Siegfried Wiedenhofer, *Das katholische Kirchenverständnis* (Graz: Verlag Styria, 1992), 279.

versality of salvation given by God in Jesus Christ or the fundamental unity of humankind. At this point, the churches do not wish to forego either proposition. If cultures can be fertile ground for the *semina verbi*, even though those cultures have been tainted by sin, then this has implications for intercultural policy within the churches. It would seem to follow, then, that in a new catholicity the churches would have to take a far more generous attitude toward efforts at inculturation than has been the case up to now. The concern about the whole and integral transmittal of the Gospel remains and will always remain legitimate. But if no attention is given to how the Gospel is being received, if no encouragement and generosity are shown toward efforts to inculturate, then communication as intercultural communication has failed. As was seen earlier, the concerns of the speaker about the integrity of the message have to be met by equal concerns of the hearer about identity. Without this, communication has not taken place. Policies that allow for little or no experimentation, that permit unilateral judgment on the results of an experiment rather than what has been called here "social judgment" (in which an extended exchange between speaker and hearer takes place) fail to be communicative in a new catholicity. To borrow the biblical image used by Peter Schineller, our attitude toward cultures and the formation of religious identities must be that we are seeking hidden treasures.[16] Failure to communicate in this fashion is more than a strategic flaw in a communication event. It is also a theological flaw, in that not respecting intercultural communication is casting doubt on the ability of the culture to be able to receive the Gospel.

A second aspect of wholeness in a new catholicity is an awareness of the fragmented and partial experience of culture by so many peoples throughout the world. This was discussed as globalized aspects of culture in chapter 3. People may aspire to live in and experience culture as an integrated whole, but globalization only increases the less-than-integrated experience, the experience of conflict, ambiguity, and partial belonging. The asymmetries of power, the experience of loss through forced migration, the sense of risk and contingency in a world threatened ecologically and in other ways—all contribute to this fragmented sense of culture. The wholeness that has been part of catholicity may well aspire to seeing cultures as integrated wholes, but there must be an awareness that such is not the current experience of most of the people of the world. A new catholicity will show a greater sensitivity to the asymmetries in the communication process. The churches try to do this already through acts of solidarity with the poor and the oppressed, and

---

[16]Schineller, op. cit.

through acts of advocacy for them. The Roman Catholic Church has done this especially in advocacy for the rights of minority cultures, a theme taken up frequently by Pope John Paul II. This advocacy needs to be extended to the plight of those in secularized societies who experience risk and contingency as well.

Most important, a new catholicity must be present at the boundaries between those who profit and enjoy the fruits of the globalization process and those who are excluded and oppressed by it. The compression of boundaries in globalization means that boundaries do not run simply between North and South, but through the middle of cities and communities. The ability to come together yet acknowledge real and legitimate difference, and the commitment to struggle with the centrifugal forces pressing down upon cultures are two aspects of the wholeness that marks a new catholicity. As has been noted several times in this book, a new theology of culture is needed. For the Roman Catholic Church, which began to articulate such a theology in *Gaudium et Spes* and has continued to do so down to the present time (especially in the writings and allocutions of Pope John Paul II), a theology of culture needs to build upon and take into account what is being learned about intercultural communication and hermeneutics, being enacted as it is in a globalized world.

FULLNESS OF FAITH

Fullness in a new catholicity is concerned with orthodoxy, the fullness of faith. Three things have emerged in the discussion of intercultural communication and the formation of religious identity that are of relevance here for understanding the fullness of faith.

The first is that far more attention has to be given to the problem of reception. If a teaching is not received, or is perceived to have been received wrongly, one needs to scrutinize the entire intercultural communication process. As was seen in earlier examples, disturbances in communication or incomplete communication may indicate previously undetected problems in the transmittal of the message itself. The helpful or harmless metaphors discussed in chapter 2 ("winning your souls for Christ") may be less than helpful and hardly harmless in a new context. Fullness in a new catholicity must attend to the reception aspect of the message. In other words, consistent failure in communication must raise questions about how the message is being sent, and not just about the capacity or sincerity of the receiver.

Second, we saw that both historical and contemporary reviews indicate that expressions of the Christian message show a continuing indeterminacy. This means that the message can be communicated via a variety of codes and signifiers. Indeterminacy, rather than being a defect, is rather an important aspect of the message's fullness, for without it the message might not be able to be expressed in some cultures. While indeterminacy may initially offend dogmatic sensibilities, it should not be so shocking when we recall that the center of the Christian message is not a proposition, but a narrative: the story of the passion, death, and resurrection of Jesus. Narrative thrives on a certain amount of indeterminacy which allows the story to be retold. Thus we will continue to encounter new modes of expression of the Christian message, as it circulates in new codes via new signifiers. In practical terms, respecting this aspect of fullness requires approaching the formation of religious identities more generously that has been the case up to now. The discussion in chapter 4 was directed toward expanding that generosity. Syncretism is often too quickly invoked without a careful reading of what is going on.

Third, the fullness of faith in a new catholicity must undertake a major theological project in a globalized world. In chapter 1, it was noted, following Roland Robertson, that the pluralistic nature of a globalized society makes it difficult to thematize a *telos* in and for that society. Global system values such as progress, equality, and inclusion can become demonic if not guided by some *telos*. The fullness of faith offers a number of theological *teloi* for a guiding vision of humanity and society. One that has been mentioned several times here is a new theological anthropology that, building on Genesis 1:26, struggles to articulate the full dignity of all human beings in a world that drives many of them deeper into misery. A second theme, articulated in chapters 3 and 4, is the possibility of an ontology of peace to counteract the centrifugal tendencies of globalization. A theological *telos* utilizing the biblical concept of *shalom* is redolent of possibilities here. The Pauline vision of reconciliation as the "new creation" (2 Cor 5:17) offers yet another *telos*.

If one is looking for the mode of mission in this third phase, then it is the elaboration of a praxis around and out of one of these *teloi*. A new humanity, genuine peace, reconciliation as a new creation—these are the forms the Good News takes in this third phase.[17] The ability to provide a goal, a *telos*, drawing especially upon the eschatological possibilities of Christian faith, is a special part of a new catholicity.

---

[17]I have tried to sketch out what one of these might look like for mission in "Mission as a Model of Reconciliation," *Neue Zeitschrift für Missionswissenschaft* 52/4 (1996): 243-50.

EXCHANGE AND COMMUNICATION

In chapter 2 it was noted that intercultural hermeneutics exhibits a number of distinctive epistemological characteristics. These will need to be incorporated into a new catholicity. There are four such characteristics.

The first is that meaning resides ultimately in the social judgment of the interaction between the interlocutors in the intercultural communication event. Thus there is a need for intense dialogue and exchange to ensure the transmittal of meaning in intercultural communication. The importance of this was already noted in the discussion of wholeness and fullness in the new catholicity. It needs to be recalled here as part of what would constitute effective and appropriate modes of exchange and communication.

The second is that truth in intercultural communication must go beyond referential understandings of truth to embrace existential understandings as well. This is an idea already brought forward in understandings of truth as orthopraxis—many cultures will not believe what one says until they have seen what one does. Because such understandings of truth are not simply an ideological choice but are deeply embedded in many cultures, the power of orthopraxis becomes even more salient for a new catholicity.

The third is the constant negotiation of the relations between sameness and difference. While attending to the requisites of intercultural communication (the negotiation of difference), a requirement of a new catholicity is attending to cross-cultural communication (the negotiation of sameness) as well. This becomes especially important in trying to articulate theologically *teloi* for a globalized world.

The fourth characteristic is an emphasis on agency in both speaker and hearer. A new catholicity requires speakers who are evangelized by hearers (such as the experience of being evangelized by the poor), and hearers who become subjects of their own history in the act of evangelization. Church policies that frustrate agency run the risk of replicating the worst mistakes of globalization and reinforcing its exclusionary and oppressive aspects.

CONCLUSION

A new catholicity, then, is marked by a wholeness of inclusion and fullness of faith in a pattern of intercultural exchange and communication. To the extent that this catholicity can be realized, it may provide a paradigm for what a universal theology might look like today, able to encompass both sameness and difference, rooted in an orthopraxis, providing *teloi* for a globalized society.

A new catholicity can meet the challenges of our time, both as a theological vision of the Church and as a policy for intercultural communication. It will provide a way of negotiating between the global and the local, recognizing the possibilities and perils of both. To negotiate that path in theology, we must be at once aware of how our world has been changing and what skills and practices are needed to understand, communicate, and act within it. Or put slightly differently by Homi Bhabha, a leading theorist in postcolonial writing,

> What is crucial in such a vision of the future is the belief that we must not merely change the *narratives* of our histories, but transform our sense of what it means to live, to be, in other times and different spaces, both human and historical.[18]

Living in a globalized world, where time and space have been compressed, where those who have and those who have not are driven further apart, a truly intercultural way of doing theology between the global and the local is required of us. And a vision of a new catholicity can guide us to it.

---

[18]Homi Bhabha, *The Location of Culture*, op. cit, 256.

Index

Theology, 1-4, 12, 14-17, 20, 25-26,
31-32, 34, 43, 46-47, 49, 52-53, 59,
61, 63-64, 68, 71, 74, 81-83, 85,
87-90, 94, 96, 99, 111-112, 114,
116-119, 126, 133; Asian theology,
2; Black theology, 2; Comparative,
31; Criteria, 63-64; Culture, 26-27,
43, 47, 53, 59, 81; Discourse, 98;
Dogma, 38-39; Hermeneutics, 43;
Local, 1, 12, 14-15, 25-26, 46-47,
87, 90, 94; Identity, 27, 63-64, 68
Tillich, Paul, 81
Time, 8, 11, 46, 55, 60, 76, 133
Ting-Toomey, Stella, 32, 35
Todorov, Tzvetan, 49
Toulmin, Stephen, 2-3
Tracy, David, 31
Tradition, 3, 14-15, 25, 28, 48, 53, 76-
77, 82-83, 86, 100; Christian 2, 60,
86, 91, 100; Europe, 86; Hermeneutics, 28; Indigenous, 77; Liberation
theology, 100; Local communities,
2; Religious, 15, 53, 63-64; West-
ern, 3
Transformation, 96-97, 117
Truth, 2, 28, 39, 41-42, 44, 46, 83,
132-133; Abstract, 41-42; Embed-
ded, 41; Europe, 41; Existential, 42;
Intercultural, 42; Modernity, 41;
Orthopraxis, 132-133; West, The,
41-42
Tylor, Edward Burnett, 49

United Nations Development Program,
7
United States, 13, 106-107

Utopia, 96-97, 100, 103, 105, 108,
113-114

Values, 8-10, 13-14, 21, 23, 29, 49, 55-
57, 78, 91, 114
Vasconcelos, José, 24
Vatican, The, 23, 77
Vatican Council II, 53, 65, 77, 79, 125,
128, 131; Catholicity, 128; *Decree
on Religious Freedom*, 22;
Gaudium et spes, 125, 130; Moder-
nity, 76
Vico, Giambattista, 48
Villa-Vicencio, Charles, 104, 110-111,
113-114
Violence, 58, 60, 77, 96
Visser 't Hooft, Willem, 62

Wallerstein, Immanuel, 122
West, The, 3, 9, 11-14, 22, 30, 41-42,
53, 66-67, 85, 87, 117
Wiedenhofer, Siegfried, 128
Wilson, Richard, 74
Witches, 33, 35, 69-70
Women, 18-20, 109; theologies, 18, 20
World Conference on Religion and
Peace, 20
World Council of Churches, The, 14,
125
World War I, 124, 126
World War II, 7, 123-126

Xenophobia, 93-94

Young, Robert J.C., 48, 52, 57-58, 77,
119